AUSTRALIA
AND
THE
PACIFIC
ISLANDS

EXPLORATION AND DISCOVERY

AUSTRALIA
AND THE PACIFIC
ISLANDS

Look for these and other books in the Lucent Exploration and Discovery series:

Antarctica
The Himalayas
West Africa

AUSTRALIA
AND PACIFIC
THE
ISLANDS

By Stephen Currie

LUCENT BOOKS

An imprint of Thomson Gale, a part of The Thomson Corporation

Detroit • New York • San Francisco • San Diego • New Haven, Conn. • Waterville, Maine • London • Munich

Jennifer Skancke, Series Editor

For more information, contact
Lucent Books
27500 Drake Rd.
Farmington Hills, MI 48331-3535
Or you can visit our Internet site at http://www.gale.com

LIBRARY OF CONGRESS CATALOGING-IN-PUBLICATION DATA

Currie, Stephen, 1960-
  Australia and the Pacific islands / By Stephen Currie.
    p. cm. — (Exploration and discovery)
  Includes bibliographical references and index.
  ISBN 1-59018-496-3 (alk. paper)
  1. Australia—Discovery and exploration—Juvenile literature. 2. Islands of the Pacific—Discovery and exploration—Juvenile literature. 3. Oceania—Discovery and exploration—Juvenile literature. I. Title. II. Series: Currie, Stephen, 1960- Exploration and discovery.
  DU97.C87 2004
  919.504--dc22
                                                              2004010685

Printed in the United States of America

Foreword

For untold centuries people have wondered about the world outside their borders. The ancient Greeks imagined that a great land called Terra Incognita existed in the Southern Hemisphere. A thousand years later, medieval Europeans were captivated by the Venetian traveler Marco Polo's tales of the mountainous regions of Central Asia and China, an exotic land he called Khanbalik. The desire to know what lies beyond what we ourselves can see is an inherent part of human nature.

But more than curiosity spurred human exploration into the unknown. Historically, most expeditions across uncharted regions were launched with practical—usually financial—goals. The discovery of a new trade route or the acquisition of new land through territorial expansion was potentially very profitable for an expedition's sponsor. In the fifteenth and sixteenth centuries, an era known as the Age of Exploration, many European nations set out for new lands and new resources to increase their own wealth, power, and prestige. For example, Portuguese navigator Ferdinand Magellan sailed along the coast of South America in search of a strait that would

allow him to bypass the stormy seas at the continent's southern tip en route to an important trading port in the East Indies. Finding a new sea passage would mean Portugal could import valuable Asian spices for a fraction of the cost of purchasing the prized goods from overland traders. In the mid–eighteenth century, England launched several expeditions from outposts in India into the Himalayas of Central Asia in hopes of establishing a trading relationship with Tibet that would allow the British to expand their empire around the globe.

Though the prospect of riches and territorial gain drove most organized exploration, many individuals who led such risky enterprises gained more in terms of personal glory, honor, and sense of achievement than the expeditions gained financially. Norwegian explorer Roald Amundsen, for example, won worldwide admiration when he became the first person to reach the South Pole, though there were no riches to exploit there. The sheer triumph of Edmund Hillary and Tenzing Norgay's first successful ascent of Mount Everest evoked a sense of awe and wonder, and a shared sense of human accomplishment, from people around the world who could only imagine the view from the summit.

Humanity has derived other more tangible benefits from journeys of exploration, geographical knowledge of the world first and foremost. When James Cook ventured to the South Pacific, for example, he charted the coastlines of many remote islands and accurately measured the distances between them. In little more than eleven years, he helped fill in a portion of the map of the world that had been empty until 1760. Thanks to expeditions such as Cook's, the geographical record of the earth is nearly complete—we know the boundaries of the oceans, the routes of the safest sea passages, the contours of the coastlines, and the heights of the earth's tallest mountains.

With each exploration, humanity gains scientific knowledge as well. Sometimes discovery is entirely unexpected: For instance, in an attempt to prevent his sailors from dying on long voyages, James Cook added plenty of fresh fruit to the shipboard diet and inadvertently discovered the cure for scurvy. Sometimes scientific investigation is a secondary purpose of exploration: For example, journeys to the high peaks of the Himalayas have yielded data on the effects of altitude on the human body. And sometimes a journey's main purpose is scientific: Deep-diving submersibles are exploring volcanoes and hydrothermal vents twenty thousand feet below the ocean surface in search of clues to the origins of life on earth. Mars rovers are equipped with sensitive instruments to detect water and other signs of life beyond our own planet. Exploration continues as humans push the boundaries in hopes of discovering more about the world and the universe.

The Exploration and Discovery series describes humanity's efforts to go to previously uncharted regions of the world, beginning with European travels and journeys of exploration, the first voyages of discovery for which abundant documentation, charts, and records have survived. Each book examines significant expeditions and voyages, highlighting the explorers—both brave and foolhardy—who journeyed into the unknown. Exciting primary-source accounts add drama and immediacy to the text, supplemented by vivid quotations from contemporary and modern historians. Each book ends with a brief discussion of the explorers' destination as it was changed by the newcomers' arrival and as it is today. Numerous maps show the explorers' routes, and abundant photographs and illustrations allow the reader to see what adventurers might have seen on reaching their destination for the very first time.

INTRODUCTION

Oceania and Its People

One of the largest and most remote areas of the globe is the southern two-thirds of the Pacific Ocean, an area that encompasses Australia, New Zealand, and the thousands of smaller islands that dot the ocean to the north and east of the Australian continent. These lands are often grouped together under the collective name of Oceania. While definitions of Oceania may differ, the term is generally taken to include island groups as far north as Hawaii, which lies more than a thousand miles north of the equator, and as far east as Easter Island, a small landmass considerably closer to South America than to Australia. But regardless of its exact borders, Oceania is vast indeed: The region takes up considerably more space than any single continent.

Not surprisingly, the region includes a wide variety of landforms and terrain. Perhaps the most obvious physical difference among the lands of Oceania is their size. At one extreme is Australia, a continent nearly three thousand miles across. At the other are thousands of tiny islets, some consisting of only a few

acres. Throughout the Pacific, smaller landmasses are much more common. The modern nation of Tonga, for instance, includes 176 islands that encompass only about three hundred square miles of land—an area slightly smaller than the land contained in New York City.

Geologically, the landmasses vary considerably as well. Archipelagoes, or chains of small islands stretching across the sea, are extremely common in the southern Pacific. The Caroline Islands and the Tuamotu group, to name two, are each made up of dozens of islands, many of them no more than a few miles apart from one another. But not all of Oceania's islands are part of archipelagoes. Easter Island, for example, is not close to any other island or island group, and New Zealand's two islands are hundreds of miles from any other lands.

The geology of the Pacific Islands creates other differences, too. Some Pacific Islands, such as Tahiti and Samoa, are volcanic in origin. They consist mainly of tall, forested mountains fringed by narrow, sandy beaches. Others, such as most of those that make up the Marshall Islands group, are atolls—low, flat islands made primarily of coral. The Australian interior is largely desert; New Zealand has glaciers and coastlines cut by deep arms of the sea known as fjords. All of these landforms and physical features demonstrate the variety of terrains to be found across Oceania.

Distance, Isolation, and the Pacific

Given the variations in size, landscapes, and geological formations, along with the enormous distances that can lie between them, it might seem that the various lands of Oceania are far more different from one another than they are alike. But in other ways, these lands have a great deal in common. Separated and varied though Oceania's lands may be, for instance, they are linked by their historical remoteness from the rest of the world. They rank, in fact, among the most isolated places on the inhabited parts of the globe. Indeed, for centuries no one beyond Oceania could state with certainty that the landmasses of the Pacific even existed.

Countless islands and islets stretch across thousands of square miles in Oceania, a vast region of the South Pacific Ocean.

The Pacific Islands

The phrase *Pacific Islands* is somewhat ambiguous. As generally used, the term does not include every island that is literally part of the Pacific Ocean. The islands and island groups of the extreme western Pacific, such as Japan, the Philippines, and Indonesia, are most often considered to be part of Asia for geographic purposes. Similarly, the Aleutian Islands off Alaska, the various islands scattered off the coast of Chile in South America, and most other islands located near continents are not typically thought of as Pacific Islands.

Instead, the phrase most often refers to the islands of the southwestern part of the Pacific. Geographers divide these islands and island groups into three basic regions: Micronesia, Melanesia, and Polynesia. Micronesia lies mostly north of the equator in the extreme western Pacific. It includes such islands and island groups as the Marshall Islands, Guam, and Kiribati. Melanesia, which is just to the south of Micronesia, encompasses the Solomon Islands and Vanuatu among its island chains; New Guinea, too, is sometimes considered a part of Melanesia. Polynesia, the largest of the three groups, consists of the Hawaiian Islands, Samoa, New Zealand, and many other lands that extend into the central and eastern sections of the Pacific.

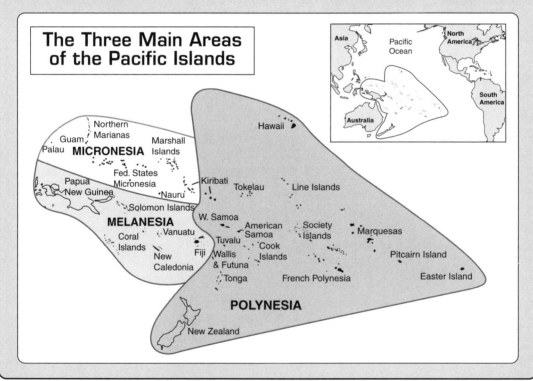

The Three Main Areas of the Pacific Islands

Two factors have created this isolation. The first is the sheer distance between Oceania and the great centers of world population. All of Oceania lies at least a thousand miles from the coastline of any continent other than Australia, and many of the Pacific Islands are considerably farther off than that. The island of Fiji, for example, is about five thousand miles from the shores of China. Until quite recent times, such distances presented an effective barrier to travel.

More important than the distance, though, was the open ocean surrounding not only Oceania's islands, but Australia as well. No land bridge connects Tahiti, Samoa, or even Australia to the great landmass consisting of Asia, Africa, and Europe, or to the two linked continents of the Americas. Until the invention of the airplane, therefore, Australia and the Pacific Islands were completely inaccessible from the rest of the world except by boat. Only the boldest and most skilled of navigators could hope to travel far into the ocean. Together, the combination of huge distances and the enormous Pacific made Oceania among the least-known places of the world.

Oceania's First Explorers

Yet despite the complications, the Pacific Islands and Australia were both explored well before modern times. At various times, at least three different waves of people left their homes in Asia and voyaged off into the unknown ocean. Spreading slowly from one part of the region to the next, these adventurers gradually settled across the region. They were Oceania's first explorers.

The Australian aborigines, or native peoples, were the first to arrive in the area. They probably reached the Australian continent some forty thousand years before modern times. The aborigines came ultimately from southeastern Asia, most likely reaching Australia through Indonesia or other islands off the Asian coast. Current scholarship suggests that they arrived by boat, although a few experts believe that a land bridge of some kind may have linked Australia to Asia during that period.

Regardless of the means the aborigines used, they were Australia's first people—and Australia's first explorers as well. Before long they had fanned out across the continent, from the harsh interior deserts to the fertile and temperate southeast. Gradually, they gave up seafaring. For thousands of years, the aborigines remained where they were, and for thousands of years, no other peoples ventured onto their continent.

The next wave of exploration began around 3500 B.C.; the exact date is uncertain. Today, these people are known as Melanesians and Micronesians, words that refer to the Pacific Island groups where they settled. These adventurers traveled by boat from eastern Asia, and they covered long distances in their trek east. Jumping from one island and archipelago to the next, they spread out across several thousand square miles of the western Pacific.

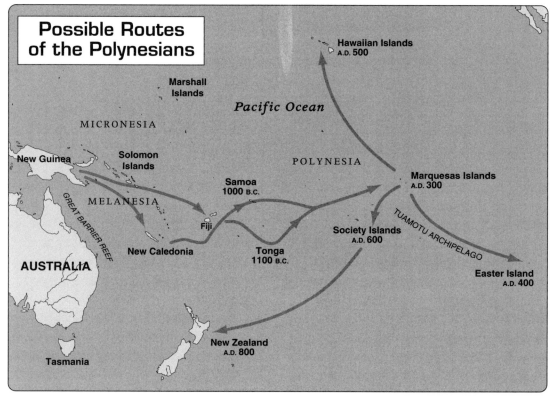

Possible Routes of the Polynesians

Remarkable as these early adventurers were, however, the most astonishing explorers were yet to come. In about 1500 B.C., a third group of Asians, culturally and racially distinct from their predecessors, took to the sea and journeyed to the east. The Polynesians were especially well equipped to make the journey into the Pacific. Though lacking engines or metal tools, they built great sailing canoes, some of them large enough to carry dozens of people. They also developed extensive navigational techniques.

Together, the canoes and the navigational systems carried the new settlers across thousands of miles of open ocean. Polynesian voyagers sailed to Tonga, Tahiti, Samoa, and beyond. By A.D. 800,

they had visited and settled nearly every inhabitable island within a great triangle stretching between New Zealand, Hawaii, and Easter Island. Some of these islands were hundreds of miles from any other landmass, yet the Polynesians nevertheless completed the dangerous voyages. Historian David Lewis has called this feat "mankind's greatest maritime achievement,"[1] and many others would agree.

Today, there is some debate about the intentions of the Polynesians. A few scholars argue that most of their longest voyages were undertaken by accident, when travelers making short trips became lost or were blown off course. Other experts, however, believe that the journeys were intentional efforts to find new islands. Either way, there is no doubt that the Polynesians brought settlement throughout the remaining uninhabited zones of Oceania. They made voyages that lasted weeks or even months; they brought with them pigs, seeds, and other essentials to make new lives for themselves. In two thousand years, perhaps less, they spread out over an area of unknown ocean larger than Russia and China combined.

Outside Exploration Begins

For hundreds of years after the settlement of Polynesia, no one from the outside world ventured into the southern Pacific. The people of the Pacific hunted, fished, and farmed, their lives and their

Latitude and Longitude

To describe the locations of places on the earth, geographers use the concepts of latitude and longitude. Each is created by drawing imaginary lines on the globe. Lines of latitude extend east and west around the world, with the equator at the center. Near the equator, these lines go on for thousands of miles; toward the poles, they are considerably shorter. These lines, also known as parallels, are used to measure distance north or south of the equator. Latitude is measured in degrees, with the equator serving as zero; the North Pole is located at 90 degrees north latitude, the South Pole, correspondingly, at 90 degrees south. The Pacific Islands lie between latitude 20 degrees north and latitude 45 degrees south.

Lines of longitude, in contrast, run north to south through the poles, and they are all the same length. These lines, also called meridians, are used to measure the distance east or west of an arbitrary zero point—a line drawn through the city of Greenwich, England. Longitude measurements run from 0 to 180 degrees. By using latitude and longitude, a point can be fixed precisely on the earth. The largest island in the Tongan group, for instance, is at latitude 21 degrees south and longitude 175 degrees west.

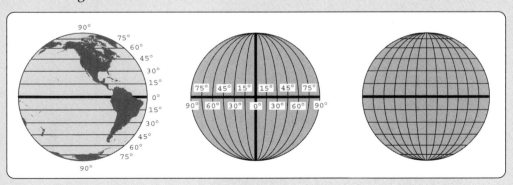

presence hidden from the people who made their homes elsewhere on the globe. But remote as Oceania was from the rest of the world, the distances and the seas could not present a barrier forever.

In the 1400s, the people of Europe began to develop ships and navigational techniques that would eventually carry them to the outposts of the Pacific. Although these European adventurers came from a part of the world almost precisely on the opposite side of the globe from the southern Pacific, they became deeply curious about what lay between China and the South American coastline. By the early 1500s, European exploration of the area had begun in earnest.

Over the next several centuries, the Europeans would follow the lead of the Polynesians, Melanesians, and the Australian aborigines. They would explore every part of Oceania, from the tiniest coral atolls to the forbidding Australian interior. They would bring with them ideas, tools, and goods that would once again transform life in the Pacific forever. For better, but also for worse, the travels of European explorers during this period would end the isolation of Australia and the islands of the Pacific Ocean.

CHAPTER ONE

Early European Visitors

The story of Oceania's exploration begins in Europe during the 1400s, a period of remarkable change. Once a cultural and technological backwater, Europe was suddenly undergoing rapid transformation. The period of the Renaissance, a word meaning rebirth, was bringing a new spirit of inquiry to the continent. For years, Europeans had been suspicious of the outside world, and its sailors had seldom dared to venture beyond the sight of land. Now, though, new shipbuilding techniques, improvements in navigation, and a growing curiosity about what lay beyond Europe's borders made longer voyages a distinct possibility.

There was good reason to make such voyages, too. Europeans longed for goods such as spices and silks, which were only produced at the edge of the known world: the far-off Asian countries of China, India, and Indonesia, the latter known to Europeans of the time as the Indies or the Spice Islands. Spices and silks, however, were scarce and expensive. They were passed by sea and by land from one trader to the next in a long and fragile chain of transactions. By the time a handful of peppercorns arrived in Germany or Spain, they might cost the equivalent of several months' earnings.

Before the 1400s, Europeans had no way to increase the supply of spices and other goods; nor could they easily lower the prices they had to pay. But with better science and technology, Europeans began to make sea voyages to eastern Asia themselves. By sending ships of their own, they could buy as many spices as they needed. They could also eliminate the traders and their price markups.

There were two potential routes to the Indies. One was the eastern route, which was pioneered by the Portuguese. This route involved sailing south from Europe and rounding the Cape of Good Hope at the southern tip of Africa, then hugging the coastline of the Indian Ocean all the way to Indonesia. By 1511, this route was well established, and Portuguese traders had become a fixture in the Spice Islands.

But one explorer, Christopher Columbus, was intrigued instead by a possible western route. According to his calculations, the Indies lay only about three thousand miles west of the European coast—much closer than traveling along the Portuguese route. In Columbus's eyes, therefore, it made sense to sail not east from Europe, but west across the Atlantic Ocean. Backed by Spain, Portugal's rival and neighbor, Columbus made the trip in 1492. And when he found land after a journey of almost exactly three thousand miles, Columbus was certain that he had found a quick route to the Indies.

In fact, he had not. Columbus had seriously underestimated the distance between Europe and Asia. Over the next few years, it became clear that Columbus had reached an entirely new land and not the Indies at all. Even so, the Spanish did not give up the search for a westward route to the Spice Islands. Throughout the 1500s, the Spanish government sent occasional explorers west from Spain, assigning them to sail to the Americas and then beyond. As these seafarers sought out the coveted Spice Islands, they would pass through the lands of Oceania. Although they would dismiss much of what they saw as of no economic value, they would nevertheless become the first European explorers to visit these uncharted regions.

A fleet of ships led by Captain Christopher Columbus crosses the Atlantic Ocean in search of a western route to the Spice Islands.

Ferdinand Magellan

The first European explorer to sail into the Pacific Ocean was Ferdinand Magellan, a Portuguese explorer in the pay of Spain. Magellan's plan was breathtakingly elaborate. He proposed to sail across the Atlantic to South America, find a passage that would carry him west around the continent, and then continue to the Indies across whatever waterway lay between Asia and the Americas. From the Indies, he would return to Spain along the Indian Ocean route pioneered by the Portuguese. If all went well, Magellan would succeed in sailing completely around the globe, or circumnavigating it—a feat never before accomplished or even seriously considered.

The voyage got under way in the summer of 1519. Right away, though, the expedition experienced problems. One of Magellan's five ships was destroyed by stormy weather and rough seas along the South American coast. The crew of a second ship deserted and sailed back to Spain, and Magellan had to put down a mutiny among some of the remaining sailors. Then, the water passage through South America—known today as the Strait of Magellan in honor of the explorer—was much farther to the south than Magellan had anticipated. Moreover, it proved long and treacherous, with swirling currents, frightening storms, and rocky cliffs on both sides. For many days the travelers wondered whether they would escape the passage with their lives.

On November 28, 1520, however, the luck of the travelers at last seemed to change. After thirty-eight days of navigating the Strait of Magellan, the passage ended abruptly, leaving the three remaining ships in a broad and apparently tranquil ocean. Magellan named this new sea Mar Pacifico, or "peaceful ocean"; today, English speakers call it the Pacific. Their spirits lifted and their hopes renewed, the crewmen set a course away from the terrifying strait. All that remained was to sail on to the Indies across this open and inviting ocean.

Into the Pacific

In Magellan's opinion, crossing the Pacific would be an easy task. Not only did the new ocean seem safe and unthreatening, but he believed that the Indies were close by. Although Magellan acknowledged that Columbus had misjudged the distance from Spain to the Indies, conventional wisdom of the time held that Columbus's estimate had not been wrong by much. Magellan thus insisted that Asia did not lie far from the Americas. In fact, Magellan believed, the gap might be narrow enough that a fast ship could cross the Pacific in as little as a week or two.

Magellan sailed north along the coast of present-day Chile until he reached a zone of favorable winds. Then he led his fleet west into the unknown ocean. The men sailed for a week, then another, and then yet another. With the winds at their backs, the vessels were making good time; still, the Indies had not yet appeared. Nor, for that matter, was there any other sign of

Ferdinand Magellan and his crew sail into the Pacific Ocean after rounding South America. Magellan is credited with being the first European to sail the Pacific.

land. Day after day, the explorers looked out across an unimaginably vast ocean, their view interrupted by nothing at all.

The empty ocean, unfortunately, was not simply a frustration. Expecting to arrive at the Indies within a few weeks, Magellan had planned accordingly. His ships carried only limited supplies of food and water, not nearly enough for a voyage that might last two months or more. Worse, some of the explorers' food proved to be rotten or otherwise inedible. By early January 1521, with the Strait of Magellan more than a month's journey behind them, the situation began to become desperate.

With their supplies rapidly dwindling, the men could no longer afford to be choosy. They began eating whatever might fill their bellies and provide nutrition. "[We] ate biscuit, which was no longer biscuit," recalled one man, "but powder of biscuits swarming with worms."[2] The men caught and ate rats that scurried around the ships; they drank water that had gone bad days earlier. Some chewed on leather. Others choked down sawdust. The foul rations sickened many men.

And still the travelers sailed west. In late January, they spotted two small islands, but neither was large enough to provide food or fresh water to the starving crew. "We found nothing but birds and trees,"[3] mourned a sailor. Dubbing the tiny specks of land the Unfortunate Isles, the men sailed on. January turned to February, and February to March; still there was no relief in sight. Deprived of nourishment, more and more men grew ill, until nearly half the crewmen were too weak to walk. More than twenty died.

The travelers' situation could be blamed partly on Magellan's leadership. The Pacific, in reality, was considerably wider than he believed, and even if his measurements had been correct, bringing more provisions would have been wise. But luck played a role as well. Through sheer chance, Magellan's path threaded between all major islands in the eastern and central Pacific. A route slightly to the north or the south would have brought them to Easter Island, the Marquesas chain, or some other place where they might have replenished their supplies. The voyagers' actual route, however, provided them nothing more than rainwater and an occasional fish.

The First Pacific Island

Finally, on March 5, 1521, the men caught sight of a new land: Guam, a twenty-mile-long island in the southern Marianas. The island seemed to offer food, water, and a safe anchorage for the weary, starving travelers. However, the people of Guam had other ideas. Intrigued by the approaching ships, people from a nearby village canoed up to the fleet and clambered aboard the vessels before the Europeans could make for the shore. The islanders grabbed every loose object they could find, especially those made of metal or rope, and returned to their village. They even managed to make away with one of the fleet's small boats, used to maneuver in shallow waters.

Magellan was furious. He ordered his crewmen to seize their crossbows and to fire on the unlucky islanders, killing several and scattering the rest into the island's interior. Magellan now gave the order to go ashore. There he and his men seized not only the boat, but also large supplies of fruit, fish, and vegetables that the islanders had gathered and stored for their own use. Still angry, Magellan and his men set fire to the village, returned to their ship, and sailed away. It was the first encounter in history between Europeans and Pacific Islanders, and it did not bode well for future meetings.

Guam was the travelers' only landfall in Oceania. Ten days later, Magellan and his crew reached the Philippine Islands, just off the Asian mainland. There, Magellan was killed in a battle with native Filipinos. The voyage nevertheless

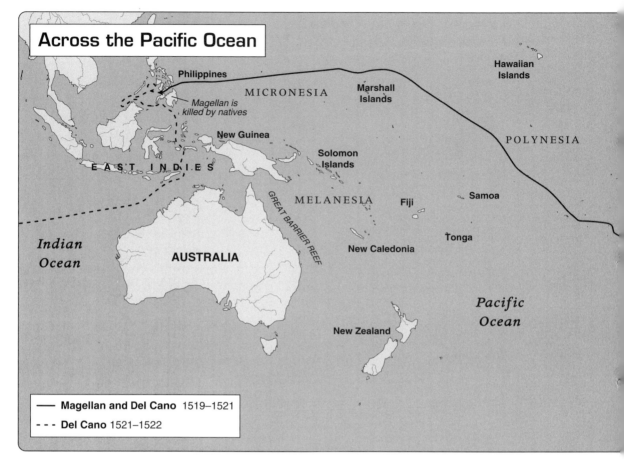

Across the Pacific Ocean

Philippines

MICRONESIA

Marshall Islands

Hawaiian Islands

Magellan is killed by natives

New Guinea

Solomon Islands

POLYNESIA

EAST INDIES

GREAT BARRIER REEF

MELANESIA

Fiji

Samoa

Indian Ocean

AUSTRALIA

New Caledonia

Tonga

Pacific Ocean

New Zealand

—— **Magellan and Del Cano** 1519–1521

- - - **Del Cano** 1521–1522

continued, with the men visiting several Indonesian islands before following the Indian Ocean route home under the command of Juan Sebastian del Cano. In September 1522, three years after setting out, the surviving members of the expedition at last returned to Spain.

Their feat was remarkable. Despite almost constant hardships, they had circumnavigated the globe. Still, their discoveries did not translate into economic gain. Magellan's route to the Indies was too long and dangerous to be an efficient way to bring goods to Spain. The Spice Islands remained an important goal; so

too did the Philippines, where Magellan's men had seen gold. But the Pacific itself seemed to have no value whatsoever. Magellan's journey had revealed miles of empty ocean, broken largely by tiny, useless islets. In the Spanish view, the Pacific was scarcely worth exploring.

The Solomon Islands

Nevertheless, in the coming decades, several more Spanish adventurers did venture into the Pacific on voyages of discovery. One of the most important of these expeditions took place in 1567.

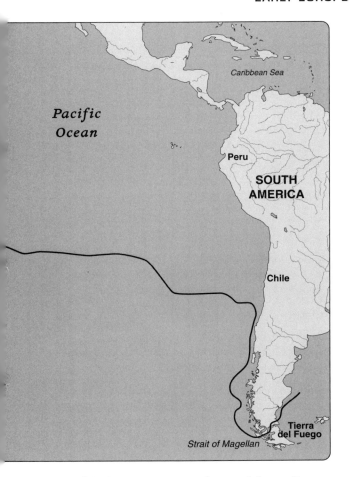

Caribbean Sea

Pacific
Ocean

Peru

SOUTH
AMERICA

Chile

Tierra
del Fuego

Strait of Magellan

This journey was planned by a Spanish sea captain named Pedro Sarmiento, but it was under the command of Álvaro de Mendaña, a young relative of the governor of Spanish-controlled Peru. Sarmiento and Mendaña had two major goals. First, and most important, they hoped to get rich. Sarmiento had heard intriguing stories from Peruvian natives about islands off to the west where gold could be found, and he meant to find it.

The explorers' second goal was somewhat less covetous; it involved geographical knowledge. The ancient Greeks had believed that a massive southern continent (known as Terra Incognita, or "unknown land") could be found below the equator. Geographers of the 1500s generally accepted this assumption and argued in addition that this continent was inhabited by people of great wealth. Sarmiento, in particular, had no doubts that such a continent must exist. His secondary aim for the voyage, then, was to look for it.

Sarmiento and Mendaña had learned from Magellan's experience. They packed plenty of food and water—and they needed both. Like Magellan, they happened to choose a course that brought them more than halfway across the Pacific before sighting any land. Even then, they could not reach the shore of the first island they encountered, probably Nukufetau in the Tuvalu Island group. Continuing west, however, they spotted a much more substantial piece of land two weeks later. "As it was so large and high," Mendaña wrote afterward, "we thought it must be a continent."[4]

In fact, the land the travelers had spotted was actually Santa Isabel, part of the Solomon Islands in Melanesia. Convinced that they had reached their goal, however, the travelers found a convenient harbor and dropped anchor. As they were preparing to go ashore, the people of the island paddled out in canoes and swarmed over the sides of the Spanish ships—exactly as Magellan had experienced in Guam. The travelers soon noted, too, that the people of Santa Isabel had the same notions about private property as did the people of Guam. "[They] went

Balboa and the Pacific

Although Ferdinand Magellan was the first European to sail from Europe into the Pacific Ocean, he was not the first European to see it. That distinction belonged to Spanish explorer Vasco Núñez de Balboa. The Spanish government had assigned Balboa to serve as a colonial governor in Central America. Part of Balboa's responsibility was to determine the limits of the land and to see whether it contained any valuables, such as gold or other precious metals.

In fact, Balboa had been posted in an unusually narrow part of Central America, where the Atlantic and Pacific oceans come within only a few dozen miles of one another. In 1513, while investigating the dense forests and high mountains of this narrow land, Balboa and his men climbed a peak from which they were able to see the Pacific. Aware that this ocean could not simply be an arm of the Atlantic, Balboa quickly clambered down the mountain and waded into the waves, thereby claiming the entire ocean for Spain. Until Magellan's voyage, however, no one had any idea how large the Pacific would prove to be.

With the help of native guides, Vasco Núñez de Balboa becomes the first European to see the Pacific Ocean.

around the ship, carefully seeking something to steal," complained Mendaña. "They quickly threw [things] overboard, for the others to pick up from their canoes."[5]

For now, the Spanish avoided major conflict with the Melanesians. Instead, they exchanged gifts with the man who led the island community, and they made arrangements to barter for more food and water. Then, they set about exploring their new find. Over the next several days, they made plans to investigate the rugged, mountainous land beyond the beaches. They also began to build a small boat that could carry the crewmen around the shallow waters near the coast.

But carrying out their plans proved difficult. The promised food was slow in arriving, and the explorers met with hostility as they tried to move up the ridges leading into the interior of the island. One group of sailors was attacked while trying to return to the safety of the ships. Mendaña had instructed his men to use their weapons only in self-defense; now a full-scale battle broke out, during which one islander was killed. Although the fracas soon subsided, the Spanish were on their guard. So, presumably, were the people of Santa Isabel.

After several attempts, the Spanish eventually found a way up the rolling sides of what they believed to be the long-awaited Terra Incognita. From the tops of Santa Isabel's peaks, they hoped to see a beautiful city spread out below them, decked with palaces of gold and silver and other precious metals. But all they could see was the distant ocean. Clearly, Santa Isabel was an island, not a continent. Disappointed, they retreated to the harbor.

Guadalcanal

The expedition was not finished, however. Over the next few months the adventurers made several shorter trips around the Solomons, which they soon realized formed an archipelago. They were particularly taken with a nearby island they called Guadalcanal, which looked to them like good farming country. The ship's company, however, included several Peruvian gold miners, and they had even

better things to report about the countryside. As expedition member Hernando Gallego recalled, "The miners said that there was gold in the land."[6]

The men had not found a continent, but gold would more than make up for it. However, when the travelers swarmed across Guadalcanal in order to search for the precious metal, the islanders objected. Tensions rose as sailors helped themselves to local families' supplies of food and water. Then, after a few skirmishes, serious hostilities suddenly broke out. Nine Spanish sailors died in an ambush, and Mendaña retaliated by burning villages and killing several natives. But despite their superior weapons, the Spanish knew they were outnumbered. Nor, after all, had they actually found any gold. Leaving Guadalcanal, they returned to Peru.

In some ways, the voyage of Sarmiento and Mendaña had been a dismal failure. Their discoveries, wrote a Spanish official afterward, "were of little importance, for [the explorers] found no spices, nor gold and silver, nor merchandise, nor any other source of profit."[7] Moreover, they had established uneasy relationships with the people of the Solomons. Gallego's description of the expedition mentions not only several major battles, but many smaller encounters in which the Spanish threatened the islanders with their weapons, or the people of the Solomons threw stones at the explorers.

However, there were positive aspects to the trip, too. The explorers made detailed observations and notes about the islands they visited. Mendaña's narrative

Spanish sailors fight with island natives in this fanciful illustration. European explorers were often met by hostile natives in the Indies.

of the trip, in particular, includes plenty of information about the animals and plants of the Solomons. On Santa Isabel, he wrote, "there are bats so large that, for fear of being accused of falsehood, I would not mention their size if they had not been seen by everybody in the fleet."[8] And despite their religious and racial prejudices against the Melanesians, the Spanish were reasonably accurate in their descriptions of the people and their ways.

The voyage added significantly to the outside world's knowledge of the Pacific

Islands. But the journey of Mendaña and Sarmiento represented a high point in the exploration of the Pacific. Nearly thirty years would elapse before another Spanish expedition would try to investigate the unknown waters again.

Mendaña's Second Voyage

The reason for the delay had nothing to do with Álvaro de Mendaña. Having experienced the Pacific once, he was eager to explore it further. Spanish officials, however, were uninterested. To them, the Pacific Islands had no value, and thus there was no reason to spend money on an expedition. Time and again, Mendaña asked for a command, only to be turned down. Not until 1595 did he convince the officials to sponsor another trip—and this journey was not mere exploration, but an attempt to set up a Spanish colony in the Pacific.

Hernando de Grijalva

Another Spanish expedition to the Pacific Islands took place in 1537, when explorer Hernando de Grijalva sailed into the Pacific from Spain's holdings in the Americas. Like Sarmiento and Mendaña, Grijalva followed a course that took him along a line just north of the equator. As he sailed, he sighted a number of islands, probably including several in the Gilbert Islands archipelago, and he may have explored one or more of these lands. Eventually, he would come close to eastern shores of New Guinea.

But that was the limit of Grijalva's success. At that point, disaster struck the expedition twice. First, Grijalva's men mutinied, killing him. Then, the ship was wrecked—it is unclear exactly how—and most of the remaining crewmen died. As a consequence, the expedition's exact course and discoveries are unknown. Still, survivors' accounts of the journey indicate that the men were the first Europeans to see at least a few of the Pacific Islands.

Hernando de Grijalva was the first European to see and explore a few of the Pacific Islands.

Mendaña's new goal was to build a settlement in the Solomon Islands. To this end, he brought with him a small fleet of ships carrying several tons of supplies and nearly four hundred men, women, and children. The fleet headed into the Pacific from Peru and traveled west just south of the equator, approximately on the same line as Mendaña had traveled years before. After five weeks, land loomed on the horizon. Mendaña confidently told his passengers that they had reached the Solomons.

But he was wrong. When he went ashore, he saw that the people of this island chain were lighter skinned and spoke a different language from the people of Melanesia. Recognizing his mistake, Mendaña named the chain the Marquesas. After gathering more provisions, he gave the order to sail on—but only after the Marquesans and the Spanish had fought, with soldiers eventually shooting and killing over two hundred of the islanders.

The travelers' next stop also appeared at first to be the Solomon archipelago. But once again, Mendaña soon realized that it was not. Instead, he had reached a chain of Melanesian islands known as the Santa Cruz. (Politically, the Santa Cruz chain is a part of the nation called the Solomon Islands today, but the two archipelagoes are separated by several hundred miles of ocean.) Weary of the journey, the voyagers decided to settle there. But angry islanders, resenting the Spanish attempt to build a settlement, attacked and killed some of the newcomers, and

a malaria outbreak killed many more—including Mendaña himself.

In October 1595, six months after leaving Peru, the remaining Spanish packed up and left. It was almost too late. They had virtually no fresh water or food, their ships were leaking badly, and they were not entirely certain where they were. Nevertheless, the chief navigator of the expedition, Portuguese native Pedro Fernandez de Quiros, managed to bring the remnants of the fleet to safety three months later in the Philippines. "They seemed like 4,000 angels,"[9] wrote Quiros of the Spanish sailors who met the weak and starving survivors in the harbor.

Quiros and Torres

As with earlier Spanish attempts to explore the Pacific, Mendaña's second voyage had met with little apparent success. Still, he and Quiros together had done some important work. They had located the Marquesas and noted the differences between the people of those islands and those of Melanesia. They had charted the Santa Cruz archipelago as well. Little by little, the map of the Pacific was filling up.

The stage was now set for the last great Spanish expedition in the Pacific. This one was led by Quiros, with a Spaniard named Luis Torres as second in command. Quiros's purpose was to find the great southern continent for which Mendaña and Sarmiento had searched without success. Like Sarmiento, Quiros believed

Doña Isabel and the Voyage West

The survivors of the ill-fated Spanish colony at Santa Cruz endured one of the most appalling voyages on record. By the time the travelers had journeyed only a fraction of their three-thousand-mile journey to the Philippines, they were out of food, out of water, and out of hope. Daily rations consisted of half a pound of flour mixed with salt water and ashes from cooking fires. Quiros described the water as "full of powdered cockroaches," as quoted in Oliver E. Allen's book, *The Pacific Navigators*. The ships were falling apart all around the passengers, their hulls springing constant leaks and their sails rapidly disintegrating. So bad were the conditions aboard the vessels that several of the colonists begged Quiros to steer the fleet into the nearest available coral reef, wrecking the ships and putting a permanent end to their suffering.

But not all the passengers suffered equally. Indeed, a handful did not suffer at all. When Mendaña died, command of the expedition shifted to his widow, an aristocrat known as Doña Isabel. A highborn lady, Doña Isabel rode in style in her own private compartment of the expedition's largest ship, the *San Jeronimo*. She also brought along her own supplies, including fine clothing, plenty of food and water, and a pair of pet pigs.

These supplies, Doña Isabel announced early in the voyage, belonged to her and her alone. She had no intention of sharing them with any but members of her immediate family. As the voyage continued, she must have noticed the cries and complaints of the starving, thirsty people elsewhere on the ship. But she ignored them. Indeed, as other passengers died from thirst, Doña Isabel used her personal barrels of freshwater not only for drinking, but also for washing her clothes.

Astonishingly, the passengers and crew did not mutiny against their aristocratic tyrant. Only when the ships staggered into the Philippines was Doña Isabel finally persuaded to help her fellow travelers—and then merely because the Spanish officials who first encountered them insisted that she sacrifice her pet pigs to feed the hungry. Perhaps lucky to escape with her life, Doña Isabel remained in the Philippines long enough to remarry. She returned eventually to Peru, where, as Allen notes with relief, "she never again plagued a Pacific voyage."

that Terra Incognita was not merely large, but wealthy beyond all imagination.

In 1605, Quiros left Peru and sailed on a jagged course that took him west and slightly south. Among his first stops was the island of Taumako, in the Duff Islands east of Santa Cruz. There the travelers met an islander with extensive knowledge of the surrounding ocean. Through signs, the islander told the Spanish that there were many large islands to the southwest. Hoping that one would prove to be the expected continent, Quiros turned in that direction. Before long, he had come upon

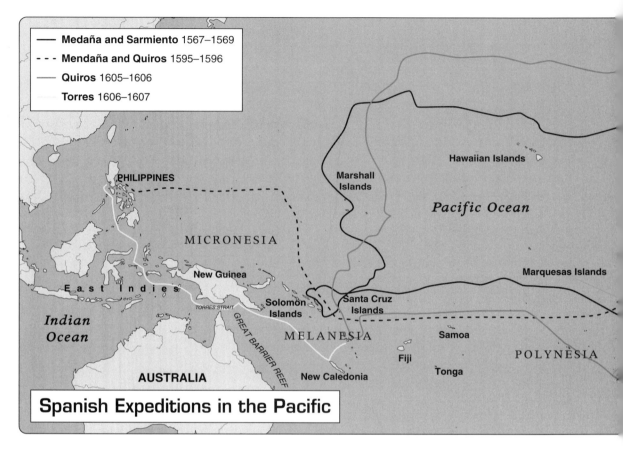

Spanish Expeditions in the Pacific

several inviting islands, but none were large enough for his purposes.

At last, in late April, the men saw a larger landmass than any they had seen since leaving Peru. It was "a great land with high mountains," recalled one officer, "which promised to be no less than continental."[10] But even if it were not a continent, the men decided, the land was exceptionally beautiful: a mix of mountains and fertile valleys with rivers and forests. Quiros steered his ships into a bay that he described as "big enough for all the fleets in the world."[11] Calling the new land Espíritu Santo—the Holy Spirit—he claimed it for Spain.

Torres Sails West

But the beautiful scenery of Espíritu Santo did not make up for the fact that the land apparently contained no gold, spices, or precious stones. And after several weeks, it began to be clear that Espíritu Santo was a large island rather than a continent. (Indeed, it is the largest island in the Vanuatu Archipelago.) At the same time, Quiros became increasingly erratic, his decisions arbitrary and confusing. In June, for no apparent reason, he abandoned the island and sailed off, leaving Torres and one of the ships behind.

Quiros and his men eventually sailed back east to the Americas, but Torres had

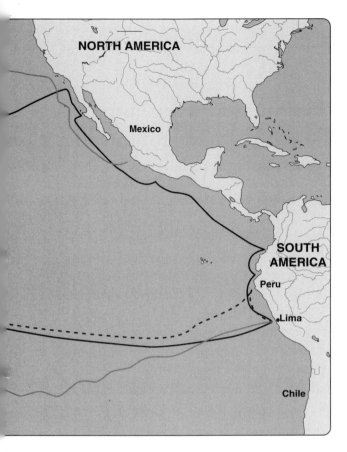

the time believed, the northern extremity of Terra Incognita. Part of his voyage, however, had taken him through a relatively narrow strait, now named in his honor, which separates New Guinea from a much larger landmass to the south. Torres's course took him too close to New Guinea to spy the headlands that made up this landmass. Though he had missed Terra Incognita, he never knew how close he had come to sighting the shores of another continent, though a smaller one than Terra Incognita was supposed to be: the continent of Australia.

The era of Spanish exploration of the Pacific was now at an end. The dwindling resources of the Spanish Empire seemed better put to other uses than steering through an apparently useless ocean. Nevertheless, the Spanish had done important work. In less than a hundred years, they had located and visited Guam, Vanuatu, the Marquesas, the Solomons, Santa Cruz, and more. They had demonstrated, moreover, that the Pacific was far larger than anyone had believed.

Most of the Pacific, to be sure, was still a blank. But then again, before the arrival of the Spanish, the entire ocean had been completely unknown to Europeans. The Spanish had begun the task of exploring the Pacific. It would now be up to mariners from other countries to discover what else lay in the great southern seas.

no way of knowing that. Unable to follow Quiros and the rest of the crew, Torres sailed west instead to New Guinea. The northern coastline of this large island had been visited by European traders, but winds and currents kept Torres from sailing along this shore. Instead, he followed New Guinea's unknown southern coast to the island's western tip, then sailed north to the Philippines.

By sailing along this southern route, Torres demonstrated that New Guinea was an island and not, as some traders of

CHAPTER TWO

Australia, the South Pacific, and the Dutch

The Spanish presence in the Pacific had focused largely on one section of the ocean. Virtually all the Spanish discoveries lay close to the equator, inside a box that stretched from the coasts of Panama and Peru on the east to New Guinea and the Philippines on the west. While the Spanish had by no means visited every island that lay in this wide band—they had missed much of the Tuamotu Archipelago, the Phoenix Islands, and Samoa, to name only a few—they had reached practically nothing outside it.

That left three great unexplored portions of the Pacific. The first lay to the north of the path of Spanish investigation. This part of the ocean included relatively little land, but it did encompass Hawaii and a few islands north of Guam in the western Pacific. The second unknown area, this one much richer where land was concerned, lay to the south. Within a few hundred miles of the routes taken by Quiros and Mendaña lay Tahiti, Fiji, Tonga, New Caledonia, and a host of other islands.

The third unexplored part of the ocean lay southwest of the Solomon Islands. The Spanish adventurers thought of this area as the extreme southwestern Pacific, but its boundaries were uncertain. At the latitudes explored by the Spanish, the Pacific had a clear end; it ran up against the Philippines, Indonesia, and mainland Asia. But no European knew just what happened to the western Pacific south of these latitudes. At some point, they reasoned, the Pacific must flow into the Indian Ocean. Perhaps a group of islands marked the southwestern edge of the Pacific, islands similar to the Solomons, the Marquesas, and other archipelagoes to the northeast. But then again, perhaps there was nothing but waves and water at the junction of the two mighty seas.

In the fifty years following the end of Spanish exploration, the focus of Pacific voyaging would turn south. A few adventurers would sail into the southern Pacific, in some cases well below the latitudes examined by the Spanish. These men were to sight dozens of islands the

Spanish had missed. Between 1600 and 1650, they would visit and describe Tonga, New Zealand's South Island, and the Horn Island group, among many others, in each case adding new knowledge to European understanding of the world.

The most important work carried out by this new wave of explorers, however, involved the southwestern part of the Pacific. During these same years, a succession of seafarers would begin the task of surveying this area. As they explored, they found themselves running into land where they had expected to find none. Over time, the truth became increasingly evident. These were not isolated islands, but different shores of one large landmass: Australia.

The Coming of the Dutch

The explorers of the early 1600s had one important characteristic in common:

Dutch explorers made several important discoveries during the 1600s, including the first sightings of the Australian continent.

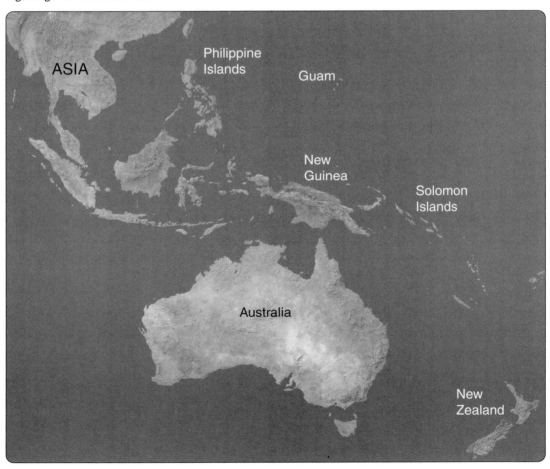

their nationality. If the 1500s were the years of Spanish dominance in the Pacific, then the period from 1600 to 1650 was equally the era of the Dutch. Their country—the Netherlands, sometimes known as Holland—may have been small, but the Dutch had a long and proud tradition of seafaring. Better yet, they were expert traders, and, like the Spanish and the Portuguese before them, trade was what brought the Dutch to the southern oceans.

Specifically, the Dutch had been intrigued by the commercial success of Portugal, which had established trading outposts all around the Indian Ocean. Once, Portugal's military might had kept other European powers out of the Indian Ocean altogether. But by the close of the 1500s, Portugal, like Spain, was in slow decline. Portuguese sailors were unable to stop Dutch ships from entering the Indian Ocean and setting up trading posts of their own. Before long, the Dutch were firmly in charge of the spice trade with the countries of Asia. And Dutch mariners routinely sailed around Indonesia, scouting for new islands with potential trading partners.

In 1606, a Dutch captain named Willem Jansz embarked on one of these scouting voyages. Jansz's goal was to investigate the shores of southern New Guinea. At first he made excellent progress through these unknown waters. Had he been able to venture just a few dozen miles further east, in fact, he would have sailed through Torres Strait, the narrow passage between New Guinea and Australia that Luis Torres would sail through from the opposite direction just a few months later.

But Jansz would never reach the strait. Before he got there, his ship—the *Duyfken,* or Little Dove—was attacked by what the Dutch later described as "wild, cruel[,] dark barbarous men"[12] along the New Guinea coast. Jansz changed course and headed directly south. Before long he encountered another coastline, this one running north to south instead of east to west. Assuming it was simply another section of New Guinea, Jansz continued to follow the shoreline south.

Jansz was singularly unimpressed with the coastline he had found. The shore was long, low, and largely devoid of life and water. The people living along the ocean had no trading goods of interest to the Dutch; besides, Jansz's crew skirmished with the natives of one settlement, and one Dutch sailor was killed. After traveling about 150 miles, Jansz gave up on the entire region and returned to Indonesia. His Dutch superiors, focused on money rather than on geographical awareness, wrote off the expedition as a waste of time and energy. "No good to be done there,"[13] one official noted.

But the voyage of the *Duyfken* was much more interesting than the Dutch knew. Although Jansz had every reason to expect that his journey south was leading him along another coastline of New Guinea, he had actually encountered a new continent. Unwittingly, Jansz and his crew had been the first Europeans to set eyes on Australia. Their voyage had taken

In 1606 Dutch captain Willem Jansz unknowingly sailed along Australia's northern coast, now called Cape York Peninsula (pictured). He believed the landmass was another coastline of New Guinea.

the *Duyfken* along the continent's northernmost stretches, a land known today as the Cape York Peninsula.

The Western Coast

In a more cooperative world, Jansz might quickly have realized his mistake. The voyage of Luis Torres later in 1606 established that Cape York could not be connected to New Guinea. A strait lay between the two landmasses, and Torres had sailed through it. But information from Torres's expedition was unavailable to Jansz—and would remain so for years. The sea powers of Europe were competitors, and Spain saw no reason to share Torres's new knowledge with their Dutch rivals. Thus, Jansz and his countrymen went on believing that Cape York was simply an extension of New Guinea.

In the meantime, however, new voyagers were approaching Australia from a different direction. The Portuguese

Dutch Exploration Elsewhere

Not all Dutch exploration between 1610 and 1630 involved Australia; nor was all of it an accidental result of ships traveling too far east while on their way to Indonesia. In 1623, for instance, two ships left Indonesia and retraced part of Willem Jansz's journey to the Cape York Peninsula, again without finding evidence that this land was separate from New Guinea. One of the ships explored south past Jansz's turnaround point. The other sailed to a long coast now named Arnhem Land. But in a familiar refrain, neither captain was any more enthusiastic about his discoveries than Jansz had been seventeen years earlier. "The most arid and barren region that could be found anywhere on earth," one reported, quoted in Oliver E. Allen's *The Pacific Navigators*.

A more successful Dutch voyage took place a few years earlier. In 1615, an expedition led by Willem Schouten and Jakob Le Maire attempted to follow part of Magellan's route from Europe across the Atlantic and then west into the Pacific. Schouten and Le Maire were intrigued by the possibility of a great southern continent. They convinced government leaders to back their voyage by stressing the markets such a discovery would open for Dutch goods—and the potential wealth that might be obtained from this new land.

The reality was less than the explorers had hoped. Although they took a somewhat more southerly path across the Pacific than their Spanish predecessors, they encountered no continent. They did, however, come upon several previously unknown island groups, including Tuamotu, the island of Tafahi north of Tonga, and a small set of islets between Fiji and Samoa that they called the Horn group. Unlike the Spanish, Schouten and Le Maire got along reasonably well with the islanders. The people of the Horn Islands, in particular, were eager to include the voyagers in their dances and feasts. In a foreshadowing of later generations' romantic notions about the Pacific, in fact, the explorers were jealous of the apparent simplicity and ease of the islanders' existence. "A life free of care," Schouten summed up, quoted in Piers Pennington's *The Great Explorers*, "like the birds of the forests."

Willem Schouten and Jakob Le Maire are welcomed by natives of the Horn Islands.

sea route to the Indies had led in a lazy arc around the shoreline of the Indian Ocean. After reaching the Cape of Good Hope at the southernmost tip of Africa, Portuguese mariners had headed northeast toward India, then dipped south again to Indonesia. The Dutch, however, soon noted that there might be a quicker way. Instead of following the Portuguese path, they reasoned, it would make geographic sense to sail directly east from southern Africa, then head north when they were south of Indonesia.

In 1611, Dutch mariner Hendrik Brouwer pioneered this new route. At the latitude of southern Africa, he met with strong winds that sped him quickly to the east. No land blocked his way. Estimating accurately when he had reached Indonesia's longitude, Brouwer turned north and arrived ahead of schedule. Clearly, the route was effective. It soon became the preferred pathway for Dutch captains ferrying goods between Holland and the Indies.

However, sea captains of the time could not accurately measure the distance their ships traveled east or west. In 1616, Dirck Hartog, heading east from Africa, misjudged the distance he had come. Waiting too long to turn north, he encountered a stretch of land—the first sighted in that part of the Indian Ocean. Hartog and his men anchored nearby and went ashore to investigate. He found nothing of any value, so he had his men carve an inscription into a plate to prove that he had been there; then he fastened the plate to a pole and left.

What Hartog had reached was a small island just off Australia's western coast, near a place known today as Shark Bay. Like Jansz, however, he had no idea what he had actually found. As far as he was concerned, it was just an island, with a few more islets visible nearby. The mainland beyond it, Hartog decided, was in all probability an island as well—larger, to be sure, but equally unpromising.

More Voyagers and a New Continent

Over the next few years, a succession of Dutch adventurers had experiences much like Hartog's. In 1618, Lenaert Jacobszoon struck the Australian mainland about two hundred miles north of Hartog's landing. Two years later, Jacob d'Edel encountered land near the present-day city of Perth in southwest Australia. And in 1622, the men of a ship called the *Leeuwin,* or Lioness, sighted a "low land with dunes"[14] below d'Edel's discovery, at about the 35th parallel south.

Still, none of these Dutch captains spent much time investigating the lands they had seen. They were in a hurry to reach the Indies, and as Jansz and Hartog had both noted, the land seemed useless for commercial purposes. While a few Dutch seafarers began to suspect that the lands might all be connected into one large continent, most simply assumed that they had come upon islands of the type the Spanish had seen in the equatorial Pacific.

But in the late 1620s, new expeditions cast doubt on this assumption. In 1627, while trying to get to the Indies, François Thijssen found himself instead at the southwestern extreme of Australia, near where the *Leeuwin* had sailed. Although Thijssen knew he was badly off course, he nevertheless was curious about the land before him. Thus, he shadowed the coastline to the east for about a thousand miles, a journey long enough to prove that this land was no small island.

Two years after Thijssen returned to Indonesia, François Pelsaert had a similar—if more alarming—experience. Carrying passengers as well as cargo to Indonesia, Pelsaert's ship was wrecked on a reef near an island off the western coast of Australia. The passengers were offloaded onto the island and the ship was either sunk or battered beyond repair. Pelsaert and a few others set off in a small boat to get help from fellow sailors in Indonesia. As he hurried north, Pelsaert followed Australia's western shoreline for about five hundred miles, becoming the first European to see a kangaroo (he thought it was a species of cat). The length of this coastline was further confirmation that Australia was no succession of small islands, but a great continent—perhaps even the one of which the Greeks had written.

Still, like everyone else who had visited the region, Pelsaert was emphatic in his overall opinion of the area. "There was no sign of running water," he complained. "The land was dry, without trees, leaves, or grass."[15] The countryside was filled with enormous anthills, empty plains, and occasional settlements of unfriendly aborigines. Pelsaert could not imagine what use might be made of it. In his view, he wrote, the whole place was an "accursed land."[16] Continent or not, Australia seemed to offer nothing of any value whatsoever.

Another Expedition

The coastlines of New Holland—the name given by the Dutch to the apparent continent south of Indonesia—certainly seemed uninviting. But as the years went on, Dutch officials began to wonder if there might be some benefit to further exploration in the area. Their main goal was not new geographic knowledge. Instead, as usual, the central purpose was commerce.

Despite the unpromising shorelines visited by Pelsaert, Jansz, and others, there was no guarantee that the rest of the great Australian landmass would prove equally bare and dry. Perhaps, Dutch officials reasoned, some part of the coast would turn out to be fertile after all. Or an explorer in the area might find a shorter, quicker passage between Indonesia and the growing Spanish market of Chile on South America's western coast.

Then there were the persistent rumors of untold wealth in lands somewhere out in the Pacific Ocean. Much of this talk centered on Guadalcanal and other islands of the Solomons, where Mendaña's men

Winds and Currents

Several factors made navigation in the Pacific difficult for the Dutch—and to a degree, the Spanish who preceded them and the English and French who came along later. The first was the problem of determining a ship's exact position, particularly with regard to longitude. This difficulty was what had led Dirck Hartog to stumble upon the western shoreline of the Australian continent to begin with, and the issue of accurately finding a location continued to be problematic for other Dutch sailors after Hartog as well.

Perhaps more of a concern, though, was the question of wind. Like the Spanish, the Dutch used sailing ships that relied on the wind for power. If the winds stopped altogether, their vessels would be left becalmed and immobile. On the other hand, if the wind blew fast enough, it could push a ship on ahead of it at a frantic and ultimately dangerous pace. Experienced sea captains knew how to improve their odds in such situations by taking down some sails or setting others in particular ways; still, the captains were definitely at the mercy of the winds.

Moreover, the winds tended to blow from particular directions. At some latitudes, the prevailing, or most common, winds blew from the west. Sailors who tried to head into these prevailing winds were forced to follow a jagged course—and typically made slow progress. That mattered both on long voyages and on shorter trips as well, especially when the direction of the current was factored in. Because of the winds and the currents, there were certain routes that a sailing ship simply could not follow.

had believed there was gold. But other unknown islands might harbor similar riches as well. Or, perhaps there would still prove to be a great southern continent. Since the people of this continent were widely assumed to be wealthy, then they would make excellent trading partners. Dutch merchants salivated at the prospect.

Finally, there was one more good economic reason to explore. By the 1630s, Holland dominated European commerce with Indonesia, and Dutch merchants were eager to maintain that edge. Dutch exploration of the area south and east of Indonesia would help forestall any other nation that might be trying to gain a foothold in the area. Even if the expeditions revealed nothing of interest, at least the Dutch would know what was there—and could use their new knowledge to keep other nations away.

Tasman and Visscher

In 1642, the Dutch decided to sponsor a new expedition to the southern latitudes of the Pacific and Indian oceans. To lead this voyage, they chose an ambitious sea captain named Abel Tasman. Born in 1603, Tasman had already distinguished himself on several important Dutch voyages, including a brief expedition to Japan and the islands just to the east. To assist Tasman, the Dutch hired an extremely able navigator named Frans Visscher. The two would make an excellent team.

The plans for the expedition were extensive indeed. The men were to start at the island of Mauritius in the Indian Ocean and head south. They were then to turn toward the east, following a path that would take them south of Australia's southern coastline—the land already encountered by François Thijssen. Once they had traveled some distance into the Pacific, they were then to turn once more and head north. With luck, they might reach the Solomon Islands. If not, there were other interesting possibilities. "We do not in the least doubt that divers [various] strange things will be revealed to us,"[17] predicted Visscher, who had helped plan the itinerary.

But the men were not looking for "strange things" so much as for conquest, trade, and riches. Tasman carried with him an official order reminding him of the expedition's true goals. "All continents and islands which you shall discover, touch, and set foot on," it read, "you will take possession of on behalf of their High Mightinesses"[18]—that is, the leaders of Holland and the Dutch East Indies. Moreover, he was expected to ask the people of these lands what goods their country produced, inquiring particularly after gold and silver—but not too blatantly. As Tasman's instructions re-

minded him, "[Make] them believe that you are by no means eager for precious metals, so as to leave them ignorant of the value of the same."[19]

Van Diemen's Land

In late 1642, Tasman and Visscher left Mauritius. They sailed south to the 44th parallel, approximately halfway between the equator and the South Pole, and several hundred miles south of the route taken by Thijssen. Then they changed course again and headed east. Visscher had made extensive study of the winds and currents in the region, and he had chosen a route where the winds were not only strong but from the west. Thus, Tasman's two vessels scudded swiftly across the sea.

On November 24, the travelers sighted land ahead. This land, however, was nothing like the low, dry deserts of Australia to the north. "Very high land," Tasman reported in his logbook. "Saw in the [east southeast] three high mountains and in the [northeast] saw also two mountains."[20] For the next ten days, the men continued eastward in a rough semicircle along the unfamiliar coastline, mapping and charting the shore as well as they could. Although Tasman decided against making a detailed investigation of the coast and its interior, he did stop once or twice so that small groups of men could briefly scout the land.

The crewmen who went ashore certainly found the land intriguing. Unlike New Holland, it was covered with trees.

Better yet, the forests contained several kinds of edible vegetables along with fruit trees. As for animal life, the men saw only the expected gulls and geese near the shore, but further inland, they noticed droppings and claw marks that suggested the presence of large mammals somewhere nearby.

The men were particularly interested, of course, in the possibility of finding human settlements. They came away convinced that people did live in the area. Several trees showed signs of hav-

In 1642, Dutch captain Abel Tasman (pictured) and navigator Franz Visscher discovered Van Diemen's Land, now the island of Tasmania.

ing been chopped as if with an ax, and smoke rose from apparent fires farther inland. But if there were people on the land, it was clear that they were carefully keeping themselves hidden. No one made themselves known to the Dutch travelers. As Tasman put it at one point, "[I] fancied I heard the sound of people upon the shore; but I saw nobody."[21]

Before long the coastline veered sharply back to the west. Tasman chose to continue east. Although the land he had just seen was in few respects like the coastlines of New Holland farther to the north, Tasman nevertheless assumed that the two landmasses were connected. He was wrong, and had he continued to follow the coast he would soon have realized his mistake. What Tasman and Visscher had found was actually a large island south of Australia. Tasman named it Van Diemen's Land after a Dutch official who had helped make the voyage a reality. Today, however, it is named Tasmania in honor of Tasman, the first European to sight it.

New Zealand

A week or so after leaving Tasmania, the prevailing winds blew Tasman and his crew toward another coastline. Large, high, and forested, it resembled the island they had just left behind, although the mountains were taller. Tasman sailed along the coast for a few days, again detailing what he and his men saw. Before long, they found a quiet harbor and dropped

Abel Tasman Claims Van Diemen's Land

Abel Tasman's visits to Tasmania, New Zealand, and Tonga were designed to increase the economic and political power of the Netherlands. Part of Tasman's assignment was to claim any land he found for Dutch use. However, this was not always easy. On December 3, 1644, Tasman and a few of his crewmen got into two small boats to row to the shore of Tasmania, then known as Van Diemen's Land, in order to stake his claim. The men brought along a stake to serve as a pole and a flag bearing the insignia of the Dutch royal family. However, the waves and winds were high. Tasman's journal describes what happened next, as quoted in Andrew Sharp's Discovery of Australia:

"We proceeded with our boat: coming close under the coast in a small bay, which stretched [west southwest] from the ships; the surf breaking so strongly, that we could not approach the land without danger of the vessel being dashed to pieces; we bade the [ship's] carpenter swim alone with the stake and the prince flag to land and remained with the boat lying in the wind; we made him erect in the earth the stake and the flag above. . . . When the carpenter in the sight of me Abel Tasman . . . had performed the work as told we having rowed with our boat as near the coast as we dared, and the said carpenter having swum back through the surf to the boat, these things being carried out, we rowed back [to the ship] leaving for posterity . . . the above things as a memorial."

Tasmania's rugged coastlines and consistent wave surges made landing on the island almost impossible for Tasman and his crew.

anchor. They had reached the northern end of New Zealand's South Island.

Tasman was hopeful of going ashore to collect more food and water. But before the men could do so, they noticed people on the coast. These were the Maori, Polynesians who had come to the island less than a thousand years before Tasman and his crew arrived. The Maori quickly climbed into canoes and paddled out toward the travelers, blowing on conch shells; some called out in what Tasman later described as "a rough, hollow voice."[22] Unsettled, the Dutch decided to remain on their ships for the night.

The next day, more Maori appeared and paddled their canoes out into the harbor, making Tasman and his men decidedly nervous. With the two ships anchored several hundred yards apart, communication was difficult. At last, Tasman assigned several crew members, including the ship's quartermaster, to get into a small boat and take a message to the other ship. But as the boat moved off across the bay, the Maori saw their chance.

Suddenly, the men in one of the canoes paddled energetically toward the small boat. Crashing violently into its side, they knocked its passengers off balance while Tasman watched in shock from the deck of his ship. Then, Tasman wrote, "the foremost man in this canoe of villains thrust a long, blunt pike [spear] into the neck of the quartermaster several times with so much force that the poor man fell overboard."[23] The quartermaster somehow survived, swimming to the ship despite his wounds, but four of the Dutch were killed in the attack.

Tasman and Visscher fought back, but the Maori stayed just outside the range of the travelers' guns. Choosing not to linger, the explorers sped north instead. Over the next three weeks they traced the western coastline of New Zealand,

Maori warriors paddle a war canoe to sea. Tasman's ships were repeatedly attacked by Maori while tracing the shores of New Zealand.

eventually crossing to the nearby North Island. At the tip of the North Island, they once again tried to make a landing, and once more, they were met with threats and hostility. The men were not sorry to sail off into the Pacific. The land was wild and beautiful, the explorers agreed, but the people who lived there were the most warlike and dangerous any European traveler had yet encountered in the Pacific.

Although the Dutch had not been able to investigate New Zealand as carefully as they would have liked, they nevertheless had some ideas about it. Clearly, it was not attached to present-day Australia; Tasman, after all, had sailed along its western coastline. But Tasman believed that New Zealand's western coast might also be the western coast of Terra Incognita. Several earlier travelers, including Magellan, had theorized that the land south of the Strait of Magellan might be a part of this legendary continent. Perhaps, thought Tasman, this was the other end of that marvelous landmass.

Into the Pacific

For now, however, Tasman did not venture directly to the east. He had found two entirely new landmasses, neither of which had seemed to harbor precious metals or trading partners, and he and Visscher now decided to cut their losses and try to sail toward Mendaña's Solomon Islands. Accordingly, they headed northeast instead.

Within a few weeks, the travelers reached the Tongan Archipelago, which had been visited several years previously by a Dutch crew. Tasman and his men stayed on these islands for a time. They enjoyed the company of the Tongans, whom Tasman said "behaved to us with great friendship."[24] But the Tongans had nothing to offer the Dutch but warm weather, freshwater, and food. They had neither gold nor silver, nor anything else of lasting value to the Dutch, and so Tasman soon sailed on.

By this time, though, the men were ready to give up the search for new lands and markets. After picking their way through a dangerous reef near Fiji, they sailed around the northern end of New Guinea and back to Indonesia. By any geographical standard, theirs had been a successful voyage. They had become the first Europeans to see Tasmania and New Zealand, and they had made extensive observations of both these lands and Tonga as well. Moreover, they had sailed completely around all of Australia, though without ever actually sighting it, and had thus established an upper limit on how large the continent could actually be. In short, they had added as much information to the map of the region as any previous explorers.

But their superiors were disappointed. Government officials blamed Tasman for not investigating Tasmania or New Zealand carefully enough. According to one official, they had left "the main part of this task to be executed by some more inquisitive successor."[25] More to the point,

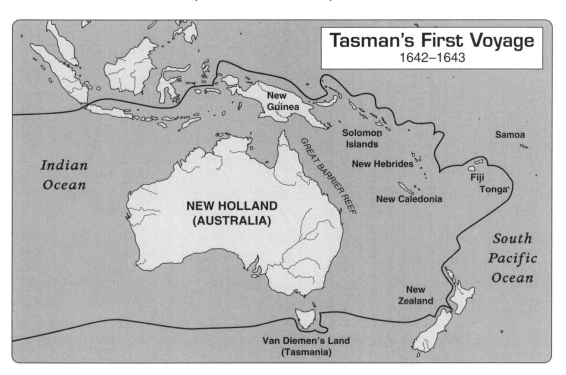

Tasman's First Voyage
1642–1643

New Guinea

Solomon Islands

Samoa

New Hebrides

Fiji
Tonga

New Caledonia

Indian Ocean

GREAT BARRIER REEF

NEW HOLLAND (AUSTRALIA)

South Pacific Ocean

New Zealand

Van Diemen's Land (Tasmania)

perhaps, Tasman and Visscher were criticized for having returned empty-handed. As officials complained, the voyage had gained Holland "no treasures or matters of great profit."[26] And that, to capitalist Holland, was the greatest crime imaginable.

An Era Ends

Despite the complaints, Tasman and Visscher undertook one more voyage. In 1644, they were assigned to return to the Cape York area of northern Australia, where Willem Jansz had sailed nearly forty years earlier, and make their way south. As with their previous voyage, the men hoped to find a passage to Chile or a civilization eager to barter. To that end, the explorers brought with

them an assortment of trading goods, including spices, gold, and elephant tusks.

The details of this voyage are lost to history. Either Tasman kept no records, or—more likely—they have disappeared. The basic outline of the journey is known, however, from a description in a letter written by a Dutch official of the time. From an economic perspective, at least, Tasman and Visscher once again failed miserably. They found no great civilizations, no passages to South America, no gold; only dismal sandy lands, dry and forbidding, and occasional aborigines, whom the letter referred to as "naked beach-runners, without riches, or any noteworthy fruits, [and] very poor."[27]

But geographically, in fact, Tasman's second voyage was almost as important as his first. He and Visscher sailed down the Cape York Peninsula till its end and then turned to follow the Australian coastline to the west. By the time they returned to Indonesia, they had reached the island where Dirck Hartog had landed in 1616, and they had covered a distance of well over a thousand miles. The two men had traced most of the northern boundary of the continent. That, combined with the discoveries of earlier Dutch captains, meant that most of the western coast of Australia had now been mapped.

Tasman's second voyage marked the end of large-scale Dutch exploration in the Pacific. Two long journeys with no gold proved two too many for Dutch officials, who refused to sponsor any more long expeditions in the region. Still, the Dutch explorers, from Jansz to Tasman, had been tremendously successful. In just under forty years, they had done major work in charting and mapping the unknown lands of the Pacific. Little by little, the blanks on the map were continuing to shrink.

CHAPTER THREE

Science and Romance

The Spanish and the Dutch had done excellent work in opening the Pacific Ocean to European explorers. But following Tasman's second voyage, interest in the ocean and its lands abruptly came to a halt. For more than a hundred years, Europeans learned very little new information about the area's coastlines, islands, animals, or peoples. Indeed, Europe's knowledge of Australia and the Pacific Ocean in 1750 was scarcely any greater than it had been a century earlier.

To be sure, a handful of explorers did sail during this time to previously unknown parts of the Pacific. In the late 1600s, for instance, British adventurer William Dampier made two voyages toward Australia, during which he briefly investigated part of the continent's coastline and sighted the Pacific island known as New Britain. Dutch captain Jacob Roggeveen, similarly, made a voyage across the southern Pacific in 1721 to 1722, during which he visited Easter Island, Samoa, and the Tuamotu Archipelago. But like the few others who ventured into the Pacific during these years, Dampier and Roggeveen were exceptions.

The reason for the general lack of interest was economic. The Dutch were not alone in their zeal to make money; every powerful European country of the time longed to find gold, gems, and other valuables—and to control the supply of these goods once they were found. During the seventeenth century and the early part of the eighteenth, as a result, business reigned supreme within European thought.

Against such a backdrop, the barren coastline of Australia and the resource-poor islands of the Pacific had nothing to offer Europeans. The great sea powers of Europe focused their attention on the nearer and wealthier lands of Africa and the Americas and left the Pacific alone. Not until the late 1700s did European interest in the area pick up again. And the revitalized interest in the Pacific had little to do with economics. Instead, the spur to explore was now science.

Terra Incognita—Again

Europe in the late 1700s was a continent that bubbled with interest in science and knowledge of all kinds. Once, it had seemed to Europeans as if the world were arbitrary and unpredictable. Now, increasingly, scientists and philosophers

The quest for scientific knowledge fueled most European expeditions to the islands of Oceania during the eighteenth and nineteenth centuries.

were discovering that nature followed certain rules and laws, many of which could be expressed in elegant mathematical equations. There was a growing emphasis on reason, the power of human beings to think clearly and logically. Reason was pure and objective, untainted by emotion or prejudice. Through pure reason, Europeans of the time believed, there might be no limit to what humanity could accomplish.

This new way of thinking had an impact on nearly every aspect of European life, from politics to art. But the emphasis on geography and exploration was especially clear. For the first time in modern European history, there was now an emphasis on gathering knowledge about the world for its own sake, not merely for material gain. Moreover, this information was to be obtained according to high standards. No longer would it be enough to estimate the position of a newly visited island or to dismiss native peoples as mere savages. Now, explorers would be scientists, responsible for making a thorough and objective analysis of the lands and peoples they encountered on their travels.

In particular, the thirst for new scientific knowledge would spark the next great wave of Pacific expeditions, a wave that began suddenly in the 1760s and continued until virtually the entire South Pacific had at last been charted. This time, no explorers or governments expected to grow rich off the results of a Pacific expedition, though none would have minded if they had. But the scientific value of such a voyage, the geographical and anthropological knowledge to be obtained, the prospect of filling in ever greater empty spaces on a map—to the Europeans of the time, these represented a more valuable treasure than any gems or gold.

By 1760, many travelers had sailed the Pacific from one end to the other. All of these voyagers, however, had stayed north of the 15th parallel south of the equator. Nothing whatsoever was known about the vast stretches of ocean between New Zealand on the west and South America to the east. Many Europeans still believed that this was the location of the fabled Terra Incognita, a

 ## The Enlightenment

The late 1700s in Europe are often known as the years of the Enlightenment. During the 1500s and 1600s, thinkers such as Galileo Galilei, Isaac Newton, and Nicolaus Copernicus had studied the forces of gravity, discovered that the earth travels around the sun, and made many important advances in the field of mathematics, along with other discoveries. Their work, though not always welcomed by conservative Europeans, did help make sense of the physical world. As time went on, more and more people came to accept the individual ideas that these and other early scientists put forward.

The work of these scientists, however, had a more sweeping effect as well. Galileo, Newton, and Copernicus insisted on looking at the world in a deeply scientific way. They observed, they recorded, they hypothesized, and they drew conclusions based on the evidence. They adopted the attitude that the world followed certain physical rules, that it was both consistent and predictable. More and more, it seemed to Europeans that it was possible to describe, to explain, and even perhaps to control the natural world.

Now, in the mid-1700s, the pace of scientific discovery continued to increase, and reliance on scientific thought and principles quickly reached a new high. The people of the Enlightenment were eager for all the knowledge they could get. Thus, the Enlightenment had the overall effect of encouraging research—if not entirely for its own sake, then for the purpose of leading to a greater understanding of the world and its ways.

landmass that might prove larger even than Asia. (Though recognized as a continent by this time, Australia was not nearly big enough to be the land about which the Greeks had written.) Mendaña had sought this continent; Quiros thought he had found it. Now, Europeans were determined to learn whether such a great landmass actually existed.

The new focus on science and reason had been particularly influential in England and France, and these two nations undertook most of the work in investigating Terra Incognita. The first important expedition was England's. In 1766, the English government outfitted two ships for sea captains Samuel Wallis and Philip Carteret and sent them into the Pacific. "An attempt should forthwith be made to discover and obtain a complete knowledge of the Land or islands supposed to be situated in the Southern Hemisphere,"[28] noted the captains' orders, which then went on to assign Wallis and Carteret the task of amassing this "complete knowledge."

These orders were carefully worded. The reference to islands indicates that the English were not willing to assume the existence of Terra Incognita. But in fact, few English doubted the reality of the great southern continent. There was plenty of room on the map for such an enormous land. In the opinion of most explorers and geographers of the time, it had been mere chance that no voyager had encountered it before. If all went well, Wallis and Carteret would be the first.

A New Land

The journey, however, was a difficult one. After a long delay to repair their vessels on the Atlantic coast of South America, Wallis and Carteret tackled the Strait of Magellan. However, the two ships became separated in a storm. Giving Carteret and his ship, the slow-sailing *Swallow,* up for lost, Wallis proceeded alone in his own vessel, the *Dolphin*. By April 1767, he was in the Pacific, with Carteret far behind.

Wallis's orders had been to cross the Pacific at a southerly latitude, but he found this to be impossible. The prevailing winds in those latitudes blow from the west, making it difficult to move in that direction, and the winds were particularly powerful in 1767. "The Wind Variable from West to N[orth] N[orth] W[est],"[29] reads the April 21 entry in the journal of George Robertson, an officer aboard the *Dolphin,* and similar entries appear in Robertson's records every day for several weeks. In the end, Wallis had to sail north nearly to the equator before he could start his crossing.

For weeks, the ship encountered no land at all. But in early June, a large landmass loomed up on the horizon. Cautiously, the travelers entered a natural harbor to investigate further. From a distance, at least, the land looked inviting: sandy beaches by the water's edge, tall forested mountains rising sharply behind the sand. The men were thrilled. "We now suposed we saw the long wishd for Southern Continent," Robertson confided in his journal, "which has been often talkd of, but neaver before seen by any Europeans." [30]

In the eyes of the sailors, this was indeed the great Terra Incognita, or at least the northernmost projection of it. But like Quiros, Tasman, and many others before him, Wallis was to be disappointed. After exploring the land both by sea and on foot, the men came to recognize that it was not a continent at all, but only an island. Wallis dubbed it King George's Island, after the reigning English monarch. Today, however, it is known by its Polynesian name: Tahiti.

Tahiti

Wallis was disappointed not to have found Terra Incognita, but he was not at all sorry to have run across Tahiti. Neither were his men. The land was breathtakingly lovely, the sailors all agreed, and rich in natural resources. "'Tis impossible to describe the beautiful Prospects we beheld in this charming spot," wrote Wallis to his superiors. "The Verdure [greenery] is as fine as that of England, there is great Plenty of Live Stock, and it abounds with all the choicest Productions of the Earth." [31]

The native queen welcomes English captain Samuel Wallis and his crew to the lush island of Tahiti in 1767.

Nor was the scenery all the island had to offer. After a few early hostilities, the voyagers and the Tahitians became quite friendly with one another. While made uneasy by the islanders' non-Christian religious customs and several other aspects of Tahitian society, the travelers appreciated the apparent freedom and simplicity of life on the island. Explorers to come would note the same perceptions. "Farewell, happy and wise people," wrote French adventurer Louis-Antoine de Bougainville, leaving Tahiti a few months after Wallis's visit. "Remain always as you are now." [32]

Still, the men of the *Dolphin* showed their greatest appreciation not for Tahitian society in general, but for Tahitian women in particular. Accustomed to rather strict Christian ideals of sexual morality, the crewmen were delighted to realize that the Tahitians did not share these notions. For unmarried women at least, there was no shame or stigma attached to sexual promiscuity. On the contrary, these women were eager to engage in sex with the visiting Europeans, and the travelers noted that the women's friends and family members seemed to encourage this kind of behavior.

The women, however, were not acting solely from sexual desire. The men on the *Dolphin* had one possession that the Tahitians craved: metal. Very quickly, the Tahitians recognized that the ship's nails and other pieces of iron could be used to make stronger fishhooks. Each sexual encounter cost the sailor several nails. It was evidently a good deal for both sides—at least until the ship's officers realized that the ship was about to fall apart for lack of nails and put a stop to the trade of metal for sex.

The men of the *Dolphin* stayed on Tahiti for only six weeks, not long enough to study Tahitian society in depth. Still, their observations of Tahiti and its people marked an important change in the way Europeans viewed the South Pacific. The explorers of earlier eras had largely been dismissive of the native peoples they had encountered. In the explorers' view, indeed, the islanders' way of life had absolutely nothing to recommend it. The people of the Pacific were brutes, beasts, naked savages.

The adventurers of the late eighteenth century, however, were not quite so quick to condemn. As their own society grew more and more complicated, they saw the value in the apparent simplicity of the Pacific; as they questioned the rules by which their culture operated, they became intrigued by alternate notions of behavior and morality. Wallis and his men reacted to Tahiti in a new and different way. Along with their scientific detachment came a new romantic image of the untamed Pacific Islander: free, pure, and uncorrupted. It was a powerful image—and a lasting one.

Captain Cook

Tahiti was Wallis's only important discovery. He continued west across the Pacific, cutting north past the Marianas and eventually arriving at the Philippines; then he returned home by way of the

The Noble Savage

In 1749, French philosopher Jean-Jacques Rousseau wrote a book in which he imagined a race of beautiful, wise, yet unsophisticated people who lived far from civilization. Rousseau's work struck a chord. To the citizens of an increasingly complex Europe, the notion of a people filled with simple wisdom seemed compelling. And when Wallis and others returned from Tahiti with tales of the Polynesians who lived there, it appeared to many Europeans that Tahiti was the very place Rousseau had described: an idyllic paradise, with perfect weather, perfect equality, and perfect innocence. In Rousseau's phrase, quoted in Alan Moorehead's *The Fatal Impact,* the Pacific Islands were truly the home of the "noble savage."

This image was not actually as close to the truth as Europeans wanted to believe. In fact, Tahitian social structure was complex and stratified. Though the islanders naturally knew nothing of Christian morality, they had moral codes of their own which could be just as strict and confining. Nor was the island as bountiful, nor the life of the Tahitians as easy, as European intellectuals assumed. Tahiti was not immune from violent storms, for instance, and wars were all too common among the islanders and their neighbors.

Images of Tahiti's "noble savages" were beautifully expressed in many famous paintings by French artist Paul Gauguin.

Indian Ocean. Wallis, however, was not the only Pacific explorer of the time. Bougainville of France, for example, who arrived in Tahiti not long after Wallis left, also crossed the Pacific. He passed by Samoa, investigated parts of Vanuatu, and eventually reached the Great Barrier Reef off the northeastern coastline of Australia.

Wallis's companion Philip Carteret, too, sailed the Pacific after finally poking through the Strait of Magellan in the *Swallow.* Carteret's crossing of the Pacific took him to Pitcairn Island in the central Pacific and the island of New Ireland just off the coast of New Guinea. But like Wallis, neither Bougainville nor Carteret had found Terra Incognita. True, none had sailed south of the 20th parallel, so there was still plenty of space for a great continent. Nevertheless, many geographers were surprised that Wallis and the others had found no evidence of Terra Incognita.

And so, British officials resolved to try yet again. This time, they sent out one of the greatest explorers in history: James Cook. A naval officer with extensive experience in exploration, Cook was a wise choice for the job. Patient and methodical,

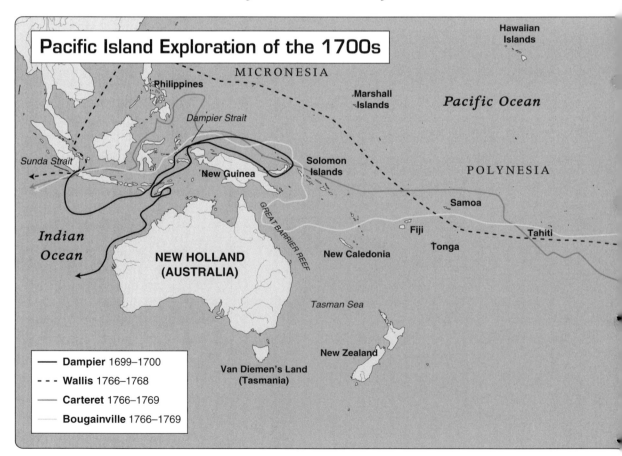

Pacific Island Exploration of the 1700s

— Dampier 1699–1700
- - - Wallis 1766–1768
— Carteret 1766–1769
— Bougainville 1766–1769

he was a keen observer and a thoughtful planner. Beginning in 1768, Cook would command three expeditions that would probe the South Pacific, the coast of Australia, and much more—and that would finally put an end to the enduring myth of a southern continent.

Cook's First Voyage

Cook's first assignment, which began in 1768, consisted of two parts. The first was purely scientific; Cook was to sail to Tahiti and make observations of the planet Venus as part of an attempt to de-

termine the distance between the sun and the earth. The second involved exploration. Once his observations were complete, Cook was to sail due south from Tahiti until he reached either the 40th parallel or, as the instructions put it, "a continent or land of great extent."[33]

Right from the start, Cook guessed the answer. Benefiting from less powerful winds than Wallis had experienced, Cook had sailed a line from the Strait of Magellan northwest to Tahiti. This route took him across miles of open sea that had been assumed to be part of Terra Incognita. Moreover, an experienced seafarer like Cook was deeply attuned to the ocean, and his observations suggested that no land was nearby. "We have had no Current that hath affected the Ship Since we came into these Seas," he wrote early in the voyage. "This must be a great sign that we have been near no land of any extent[,] because near land are generally found Currents."[34]

Cook enjoyed his time in Tahiti. Following the close of his assignment, he and his crew spent several days charting Tahiti's coast and investigating some smaller islands nearby. At one point, several members of the crew picked their way into the interior of one of the islands and partway up a mountain. Next, Cook zigzagged southward across the Pacific. By the time the men reached the 40th parallel, they were deep inside uncharted ocean. But there was no sign of any land at all, continent or otherwise. Following his instructions, Cook turned now to the west and made for New Zealand instead.

English captain James Cook spent the better part of eleven years traversing the Pacific Ocean in search of new lands and knowledge.

Cook had dealt a great blow to the notion that Terra Incognita existed in the central Pacific. Now he exploded the idea that New Zealand was a part of the southern continent. Between October 1769 and March 1770, Cook circled both islands of New Zealand, sailing around their coasts and through the narrow strait that divides the islands from one another. In five months, he charted about twenty-four hundred miles of coastline. By the time the ship had completed its circuit, it was clear that New Zealand was unconnected to a larger landmass.

Cook's official assignment was at an end. Now it was time for him to return home.

There was an argument to be made for sailing east across the Pacific. The winds would be favorable, and the voyage might shed more light on the existence—or lack thereof—of the great but rapidly shrinking southern continent. But Cook rejected the idea. Winter was coming, and he was not certain that his ship would withstand the journey through the Pacific storms. Besides, Cook had a yearning for more adventure.

To Australia

Instead, Cook chose to sail west to the shores of Australia, or New Holland as it still was called, and to explore its unknown eastern shore. In April 1770, he arrived at the southeastern corner of Australia and began making his way north. He immediately noticed that this section of Australia was notably different from the dry and bare sections explored by the Dutch. "The face of the country is green and woody,"[35] Cook wrote, and he was right: He had stumbled across one of the few temperate sections of the continent.

Unlike Tasman, who preferred to make observations from the deck of his ship, Cook stopped often to land. He was the first visitor to Australia to spend much time on the shore. Indeed, Cook and his men frequently struggled up hills and mountains to make careful records of the land and the nearby seas. Cook, moreover, was much more interested in the natural history of the places he visited than earlier explorers had been. The men of his expedition made thorough observations of the region's people, plants, and animals, including dingoes, wallabies, and kangaroos. Thus, the travelers moved along slowly.

By August, however, Cook had at last reached the northernmost point of Australia: the tip of the Cape York Peninsula, directly south of Torres Strait and New Guinea. Cook and his men had traversed nearly fifteen hundred miles of Australia's eastern coast. It was an appropriate cap to a remarkable voyage. Cook had explored thousands of square miles of the South Pacific, proved that New Zealand was actually a pair of islands, and charted the entire eastern shoreline of Australia. The detail and breadth of his information about Australia and the Pacific was unrivaled by any explorer before him. He returned to England to wide acclaim.

Another Expedition

A few scientists, however, were less than fully satisfied by Cook's findings. Their main concern was with Cook's conclusion that Terra Incognita did not exist. These men charged that Cook had given up the search too easily. Although Cook was not swayed by the argument, he did concede that he had not proved his point. So he proposed a new expedition, one that, as he phrased it, would "put an end to all diversity of opinion about a matter so curious and important." [36] In 1772, Cook sailed from England on an expedition that would last just over three years.

Kangaroos were first seen by Cook and his men during an observational landing on Australia in 1770.

It was in some ways the most remarkable expedition ever attempted by any explorer. Cook spent most of these three years crisscrossing the southern Pacific from New Zealand to the east. He penetrated through the sub-Antarctic ice as far south as the 71st parallel, and he made multiple horizontal and vertical sweeps of the ocean to the north, all without finding any sign of Terra Incognita. By the time he had finished, there could no longer be any doubt in anyone's mind. "No continent was to be found in this ocean," Cook stated flatly, "but what must lie so far to the south as to be wholly inaccessible on account of ice."[37]

If this conclusion had been the only outcome of Cook's adventure, it would still have been an impressive journey. But Cook did much, much more. "Although I had proved there was no Continent," he wrote, "there remained room for many large Islands [within the southern Pacific], in places wholly unexplored[,] and many of these formerly discovered are but imperfectly explored."[38] Accordingly, the travelers set out to find as many new islands as possible—and to improve knowledge about ones visited a century or so earlier.

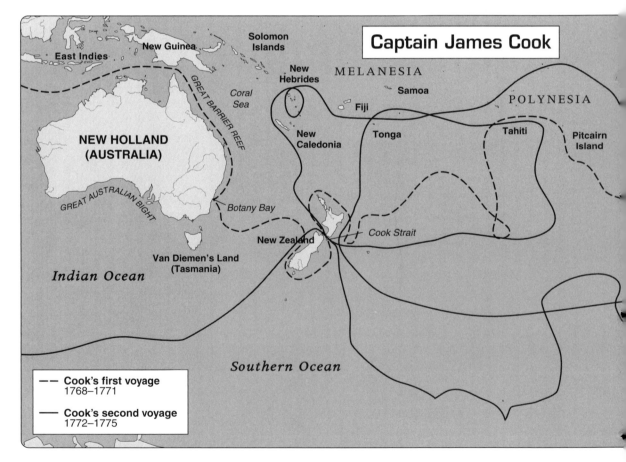

The Last Pacific Islands

It was a tall task, but Cook and his voyagers were equal to it. Their travels took them back to Tahiti and New Zealand, where they carried out further studies of the lands and the people. They made brief visits to Easter Island, Tonga, and various parts of the Marquesas chain; each had been explored by earlier European adventurers, but Cook was able to locate their positions more accurately than anyone before him. And they spent several weeks in Vanuatu, where they made detailed charts of the coastline, investigated the interiors of the islands, and took careful notes on people, animals, and plants.

Moreover, Cook and his men sighted and mapped dozens of previously unknown islands. Many of these, to be sure, were tiny, but others were inhabited and quite large. Among these was the island of New Caledonia, one of the biggest in the South Pacific. Cook spent about three weeks at this island, getting to know the people and charting several hundred miles of the coastline. Although New Caledonia had few resources, the travelers found the natives friendly and welcoming. As one member of the expedition put it, "The Natives are the most harmless & goodnatured Set of people, that we have as yet met with."[39]

Cook returned to England with proof that there was no southern continent. He also brought back pages and pages of information about the lands, the peoples, and the natural history of the South Pacific. He had done his work so well, in fact, that very little about the map of the Pacific now remained unknown. Distances, coastlines, relative positions—all were rapidly being filled in.

Only one major Pacific Island chain remained unknown to Europeans of the time, and Cook soon took care of that. In 1777, he began his third and last expedition, this one primarily focused on the extreme northern Pacific. He did find time to visit Tahiti, however; and while sailing directly north from this island, Cook unexpectedly encountered the Hawaiian Islands more than a thousand miles above the equator.

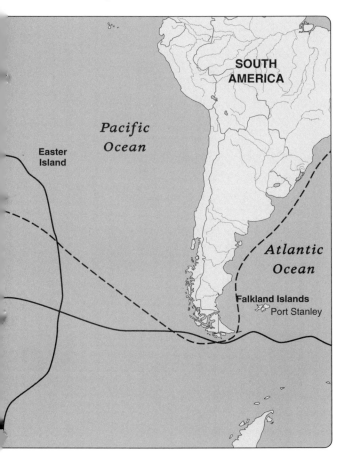

Hurrying to reach the far northern Pacific before the onset of winter, Cook did not dare spend too much time in Hawaii. Nevertheless, he stopped briefly to investigate the area before sailing on. Cook called the chain the Sandwich Islands after one of his sponsors, an English nobleman known as the Earl of Sandwich, and promised to return the following year for further exploration.

The decision to return would cost Cook his life. Cook had always been notable for the respect with which he had treated the peoples of the Pacific. Like few other explorers, he understood perfectly well why he and his ships might be greeted with hostility. He saw clearly that the inhabitants perceived the explorers to be invaders of their lands.

But in Hawaii, Cook lost his patience. When islanders threw stones at the sailors, he ordered his men to shoot into their midst. Tempers flared on both sides before the two sides reached an uneasy

 Island Names

Most Pacific Islands have been known by several different names over the years, a fact that makes it hard to keep them straight. Many of these islands were originally named by the first European explorers to find them, and most of the names they gave out were in honor of sponsors, saints, or other lands at home. Thus, the map of the Pacific includes many European names such as Santa Isabel, the Horn Islands, and New Caledonia.

This practice was confusing, however. Explorers of different nationalities sometimes gave the same island different names, making it hard to tell which island was which. Among the men who disapproved of this practice was Johann Reinhold Forster, a naturalist who accompanied James Cook on his second voyage. "Had all the former Navigators taken the prudent Step to inquire of the Natives, for the Names of the Islands they saw," he wrote in his *Resolution Journal of Johann Reinhold Forster,* "we might be able to ascertain with certainty, what are new discoveries and what are not." (Cook himself, however, was often eager to choose his own names for islands, among them New Caledonia and the Sandwich Islands for Hawaii.)

In some cases, Forster's wishes were followed. After a short period of being called King George's Land, Tahiti became known by a variation of Otaheite, its Polynesian name. Fiji also was called Fiji from early on. Others, however, have had to reclaim their names. Some, like Hawaii (named the Sandwich Islands by Cook) and Tonga (the Friendly Islands to Europeans), have been known by their traditional names for more than a century; other islands, such as Kiribati and Tuvalu, have made the change more recently. Nevertheless, many Pacific Islands—among them the Solomons, the Marianas, and New Zealand—are known even today by their European names.

Captain James Cook is killed by native Hawaiians during a fierce battle in 1779.

truce. When several Hawaiians made off with one of the small boats belonging to Cook's ship, however, Cook became furious. He retaliated by taking a Hawaiian dignitary hostage—some sources suggest it may have been the local king—and giving orders to bring the prisoner out to the English ship as it lay in the harbor.

But the Hawaiians had other plans. Despite the English advantage in weaponry, a crowd of irate natives gathered on the shore. Prepared to use force if necessary to free the prisoner, the Hawaiians threatened the Europeans with spears and rocks. A scuffle began and soon escalated into violence. By the time the hostilities were over, a number of Hawaiians lay dead on the beach, joined by several of Cook's men—and by Cook himself, stabbed by the mob as he stood on the rocks at the edge of the shore.

Cook's death was an ignoble end to a great career and a remarkable life. Still, Cook's third voyage had once more added to European knowledge of the Pacific. Before Cook, the Pacific was still largely unknown; dozens of its islands had never been visited by Europeans. During Cook's three voyages, however, that situation changed considerably. By the time of his death, European exploration of the region was essentially at an end. At last, all the major island groups were known to the outside world. Thanks in large part to Cook's efforts, the vast ocean was a mystery no more.

CHAPTER FOUR

Investigating Australia

With exploration of the South Pacific more or less at a close, the attention of England shifted to Australia. By the 1780s, the continent was not totally unknown. At one time or another, Cook, Tasman, and several other explorers had sailed along most of the land's coastlines and collected valuable information on Australia's basic shape and size. A few of the explorers, notably Cook, had gone ashore, and several had encountered the aborigines living there.

Still, much about Australia remained unclear. The interior was completely unknown; no one had ventured much beyond the beaches. Several stretches of coastline had not been investigated at all, most notably the eastern half of the continent's southern shore. And the rest of the coastline was known in outline only. The Dutch, in particular, had kept their distance from the rocky and potentially dangerous coasts. Thus, they had missed some of the inlets, promontories, and other features of Australia's shore. For all earlier explorers knew, a long strait might split the land in two parts.

Until the 1780s, this lack of information was not a serious problem. Except for a stretch of the southeastern coast explored by Cook, after all, the entire Australian continent seemed to have no value. But as 1800 approached, two factors encouraged further exploration. The first was the continuing thirst for knowledge. The second was southeastern Australia's new status as the British colony of New South Wales—used first for housing prisoners, and later as a place where free English citizens immigrated as well.

Together, these factors led to an explosion of interest in Australian geography. Between 1800 and 1830, the Australian coast was thoroughly charted at last, the southeastern fringes of the interior were explored, and the mystery of Australia's rivers was resolved. Much would remain unknown even after these years, but the brave British explorers of the early nineteenth century would nonetheless add valuable information to world understanding of Australia.

Matthew Flinders

The first task was to obtain an accurate map of Australia's coast. For that, the English government called on Matthew Flinders. Flinders had originally intended to become a doctor, but when he read *Robinson Crusoe,* Daniel Defoe's classic tale of a castaway on a deserted island, Flinders decided to become a sailor instead. In 1798, he received his first major Australian assignment: to determine whether Tasmania was an island or a part of Australia's mainland.

Few mariners who had sailed in the area believed that Tasmania was an island. True, the Pacific emptied into a large unexplored inlet along Tasmania's northeastern shore. But it was generally assumed that this body of water was only a gulf, not a passage between Tasmania and the continent to its north. When Flinders steered into the supposed gulf, however, he sailed into the Indian Ocean on the opposite side, thus demonstrating that Tasmania and Australia were unconnected. "[We] hailed [our discovery] with joy and mutual congratulation," Flinders recalled later, "as answering the

Prisoners bound for New South Wales are caged below deck on a transport ship. Many British prisoners and undesirables were shipped from Europe to Australia.

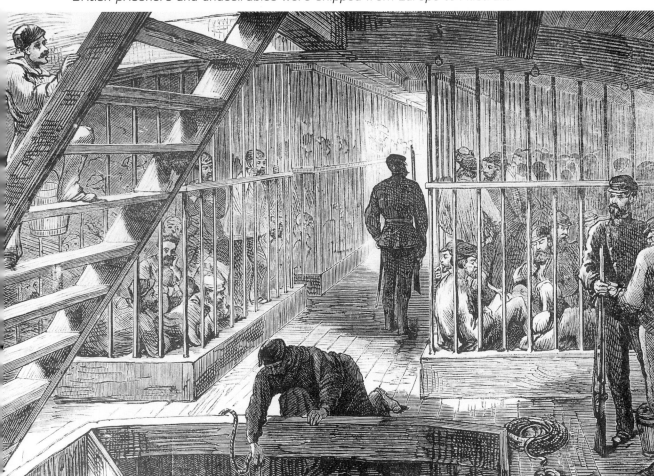

long-wished-for discovery of a passage into the Indian Ocean."[40]

But Flinders was not content to stop with Tasmania. Next, he badgered the English government into sending him on a second and far longer voyage: a complete circumnavigation of Australia. England agreed, as the British were eager to continue their quest for knowledge. They also hoped to forestall their archrival, France, which was interested in setting up Australian colonies of its own. Whatever Flinders could learn about the continent would help strengthen England's claim to the land.

Flinders was a careful and deliberate man, and his planning reflected that. "My greatest ambition," he wrote, "is to make such a minute examination of this extensive and very interesting country that no person shall have occasion to come after me to make further discover-

New Zealand's Interior

Although the greatest share of Pacific exploration ended with Cook's third voyage, there were nevertheless a few places still to be investigated. Some of the northernmost islands of the Marianas group, for instance, remained unknown to outsiders until an American sea captain arrived there in 1791. But the largest empty stretch of the map after Cook was the interior of New Zealand.

Although New Zealand is much smaller than Australia, the interior of the continent did present several important challenges to explorers. The land is rocky and mountainous, and the South Island in particular is subject to extremes of temperature that can make traveling difficult, especially at higher elevations. During the 1800s, a few British explorers—in nearly all cases led by Maori guides—ventured into the interior of the two islands to see what was there.

Among the first to explore the more tropical North Island were two brothers, William and Henry Williams. Both men were missionaries, in charge of a wide area of sparsely populated land, and both spent considerable time traveling around their domains. Henry Williams was particularly interested in exploration. In 1839 and 1840, he trekked across the island, at various times climbing sheer cliffs and paddling a canoe up rushing rivers. Two years later, an amateur scientist named William Colenso made another extensive trip through the North Island, recording what he observed about the plants and animals. All these men added to the knowledge of the island and its terrain.

The most important explorer on the South Island was another Englishman, this one named Thomas Brunner. Brunner was part of several expeditions to the island's coastline and interior. These were by far the most dangerous and dramatic expeditions of New Zealand following Cook; Brunner nearly froze to death during one of the trips, and he nearly starved during another. Still, the completed surveys brought back important information about the island and its resources.

ies."[41] It was a rather grand ambition, but Flinders was clear: Unlike several earlier explorers, he would be concerned with accuracy, not speed. He would follow every inlet, describe every headland, examine every offshore isle. He would put together the definitive map of the Australian coastline, he was sure, and there would never again need to be another expedition to investigate Australia by sea.

Around the Continent

In 1801, Flinders arrived in Australia's southwestern corner, near where the Dutch captain François Thijssen had sighted the continent nearly two centuries before. He first headed east, examining the shoreline as he did so. For the first thousand or so miles, he was simply following in Thijssen's path, though more systematically and probably much closer to the coastline. But before long, the travelers reached a stretch along which no European ship had ever sailed.

Now Flinders was in his element. He plodded along, recording every natural feature he found; nothing seemed too small to escape his attention. He gave names to hundreds of points, bays, and islands. Most he named for his crewmen or his government backers, but not all. Flinders's map of Australia's southern coast included Smoky Bay, Streaky Bay, and Denial Bay, the last named for "the deceptive hope we had . . . of penetrating by it some distance into the interior country."[42]

Flinders completed his survey of the southern coast without major problems; then he swung north along the eastern coast of Australia. James Cook had already done a fine job of charting this shoreline, but Flinders nevertheless added new information and cleared up some uncertainties. "I saw not only that Cape Townshend was on a distinct island," he wrote about one of several places Cook had sighted but not thoroughly explored, "but also that it was separated from a piece of land to the west, which captain Cook's chart had left doubtful."[43] He sailed up the Cape York Peninsula and through Torres Strait at the top of the continent. Once again, he was in a part of Australia that had been investigated only by the Dutch.

But here, Flinders encountered problems. His ship was old and leaky, and the carpenters in the crew cautioned him that it could no longer be repaired. Flinders was bitterly disappointed. "I find the complete examination of this extensive country, which is one of the nearest objects of my heart, to be greatly impeded, if not wholly frustrated,"[44] he wrote in despair. Flinders tried to continue the detailed survey anyhow, but by the time he was halfway across the continent's northern coast it was clear that the ship could no longer withstand the stresses of sailing so close to the shore.

Reluctantly, Flinders gave up. Instead of poking along near the coast, he opted for caution instead. Sailing in a wide arc around the northwest corner of the continent, he headed down Australia's western edge and completed his

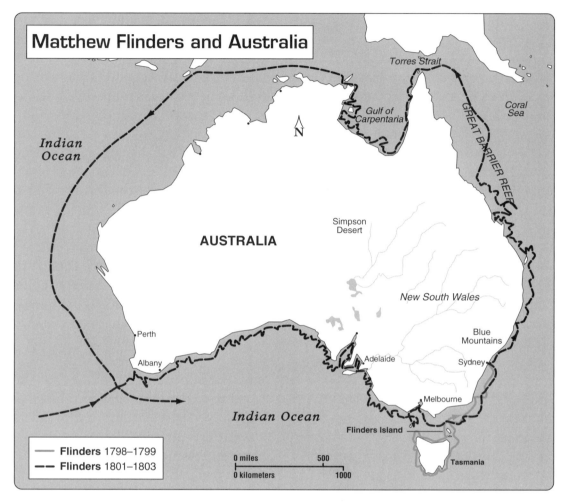

Matthew Flinders and Australia

Torres Strait

Coral Sea

Gulf of Carpentaria

GREAT BARRIER REEF

Indian Ocean

N

AUSTRALIA

Simpson Desert

New South Wales

Perth

Blue Mountains

Albany

Adelaide

Sydney

Melbourne

Indian Ocean

Flinders Island

— Flinders 1798–1799
--- Flinders 1801–1803

0 miles 500
0 kilometers 1000

Tasmania

circumnavigation—but without the opportunity to examine the entire coast as closely as he would have liked. Still, Flinders had more than done his job. He had added tremendously to the map of Australia. He had demonstrated that no large body of water cut the continent in two. Like Cook, he returned to England with copious notes on Australian geology, botany, and anthropology. Most important, perhaps, he had carried out his stated goal: His was to be the last major investigation of Australia by sea.

The Blue Mountains and Beyond

With the Australian coastline well charted, attention now turned to the country's rugged interior. England had chosen one of the most temperate parts of Australia's coastline for its New South Wales colony, and the region was reasonably fertile as well. More and more people were arriving each month to start a new life there. But the colony had no room to grow. It was hemmed in by the Blue Mountains a few dozen miles inland.

The Blue Mountains were not especially high, but the peaks were jagged and the underbrush was thick. Progress through this barrier was difficult—so difficult, in fact, that an early colonial governor called the mountains "impassable" and derided plans to cross them as "useless."[45] Indeed, the first few explorers to make the attempt turned back in disgust. Not until 1813 would an expedition led by a colonial rancher, Gregory Blaxland, prove the governor wrong.

To be sure, Blaxland's expedition was difficult. His progress was agonizingly slow: He and his two companions averaged just three miles a day. Nor did the travelers ever descend into the valley on the other side of the range. But they did reach a point from which they could see down onto the prairies to the west of the mountains. These lands were vast and fertile—"sufficient," as one of Blaxland's companions put it, "to support the [live]stock of the colony for the next 30 years."[46]

Blaxland's information sparked a flurry of interest in this new land. Over the next few years, several more explorers tried to learn more about the lands to the west of the new colony. George Evans, the first to actually reach the prairies, pressed on farther west once he arrived and stumbled upon a large river which he named the Lachlan. A few years later, John Oxley went further still. Venturing to the north of Evans's route, he found another river, which he called the Macquarie. Then he returned to the coast by another route.

Unfortunately, the prairie did not seem to extend very far to the west. The Lachlan and the Macquarie both flowed west, but when Evans and Oxley tried to follow them, they found that each river soon flowed into thick, barely navigable swamps. Both explorers were disappointed. Returning to New South Wales,

The daunting Blue Mountains (pictured) were considered an impassable obstacle by New South Wales colonists until Gregory Blaxland's 1813 expedition.

Oxley asserted that the swamp was just one end of a huge inland lake, shallow and overgrown and "unprofitable to man and beast."[47] Most colonists agreed—but not all.

The Murray and the Murrumbidgee

The next great task of Australian exploration would be to test Oxley's assumption. The first to try were two British explorers, Hamilton Hume and William Hovell. In 1824, they led a small expedition into the interior of New South Wales. The colony's governor wanted them to blaze an overland trail to Australia's southern coast. Thus, rather than heading directly west into the mountains, they quickly veered to unexplored territory to the south.

The journey lasted about three months. Its results were mixed. On the positive side, Hume and Hovell found extensive flatlands as they made their way south, lands that they thought would be good for grazing sheep and other livestock. On the other hand, the path did not prove to be a convenient shortcut between the coasts. In places, rocky cliffs made the going difficult; in others, the men had to hack their way through thick underbrush. Worse, much of their route seemed infested with ticks, mosquitoes, and other pesky insects. But Hume and Hovell had succeeded in charting and investigating many miles of unknown territory, and that was an achievement in itself.

The journey was also noteworthy for the information Hume and Hovell brought back about two important rivers. The more northerly of the two was the Murrumbidgee, which had been sighted, though not explored, by an earlier adventurer. The more southerly of the two is known today as the Murray. It was springtime in the Southern Hemisphere when the men encountered each of the rivers for the first time, and that meant flood season. Both rivers were wide, wild, and raging. To cross the Murray, in fact, the men were forced to make a small boat out of tarpaulins and load their equipment on it. The travelers then swam across the current, pulling the contraption along by a rope.

Hume and Hovell had no time to explore the rivers. They were heading south, and the rivers were flowing west. But they were intrigued by the size of the rivers, as well as by the fact that both rivers ran in the same direction as the Lachlan and the Macquarie. Now there were four large interior rivers known to the British, and all of them flowed in the same general direction. The question was what happened to them. Perhaps they all drained into the same swamp; perhaps the swamp was truly an inland sea, as Oxley had supposed. Or perhaps the two new rivers eventually drained into the ocean. No one knew.

Sturt, Hume, and the Darling

In 1828, Hume decided to find out. He embarked on another expedition, this

Natives help an explorer cross a river using handmade boats and rope. Crossing fast-moving rivers and streams with large supply loads was a serious problem for many overland expeditions in Australia.

time with a British soldier named Charles Sturt serving as his partner. Sturt and Hume traced Oxley's route along the Macquarie. But their experience was vastly different from what Oxley's had been. Where Oxley had found a massive swamp, Sturt and Hume found little water, just land with a covering of dried mud. It soon became apparent that the swamp only existed in wet weather. Oxley had happened upon the area during one of the rainiest winters on record. Sturt and Hume, in contrast, had arrived during a hot summer following a dry winter.

In some ways, the dryness was an advantage to exploration. The surface of the land was readily available for Hume and Sturt to study as they pleased. The men needed no boat to travel, and there was no difficulty finding suitable places to camp. But in other ways, the lack of a swamp presented a serious problem for the travelers. Most notably, water was scarce. The men sometimes had to squeeze moisture out of the mud to quench their thirst. Tall reeds formed a barrier to travel, too, and the insects were as bad here as they had been on Hume's earlier trek.

Still, the men pressed on. In February 1829, they suddenly came upon yet another river—the Darling. Despite the dryness of the land around it, the Darling was a "noble river," Sturt wrote, "70 to 80 yards broad."[48] This river flowed southwest, which carried it toward the same basic place as the Macquarie and the other recently explored rivers. Sturt and Hume would have gladly followed it downstream, but they did not dare. Though to the best of their knowledge the ocean was miles away, the water was nevertheless salty—as it turned out, the result of nearby salt deposits. Hume and Sturt knew they had barely enough freshwater to get them back to New South Wales. Reluctantly, they turned around and headed for home, the great question remaining unanswered.

Now explorers knew of five major rivers in southeastern Australia—and no one had any idea where they eventually drained. "[The Darling's] course is involved in mystery," Sturt wrote—but his words could have referred to any of the other four rivers as well. "Does it make its way to the south coast, or exhaust itself in feeding a succession of swamps in the center of the island [that is, Australia]?"[49] On the whole, Sturt leaned toward the second explanation. But he kept an open mind. Someday, he hoped, he would have a chance to find the truth.

Sturt's Second Expedition

Sturt got the chance, and sooner than he had expected. Later in 1829, he was asked to head up an expedition down the Murrumbidgee. This was a complicated undertaking. The first part of the journey would be overland; then, assuming there was enough water in the river channel, the men would need to have a boat. Accordingly, Sturt brought along a disassembled boat, twenty-seven feet long. When the men reached the Murrumbidgee, they quickly put it together—along with constructing a second, smaller boat from the wood of a nearby tree.

Sturt's plan was to take some of the men down the Murrumbidgee in the boats. The larger boat would hold the travelers, the smaller would be used for provisions. Several of the men, though, were to stay at the base, where the boats were being constructed. Sturt had no clear idea where the river would take him; for all he knew he would soon run into an impassable swamp as he had done with Hume a year earlier. In case he had to retrace his footsteps, he decided, it would be good to have assistance waiting at the base.

On January 7, 1830, the travelers departed. At first the men made their way through heavy plant life. "Reeds lined the banks of the river on both sides without any break," he wrote, "and waved like gloomy streamers over turbid [muddy] waters."[50] But as the men traveled downstream, the channel opened. Now, the current moved the boats along rapidly—in some cases, entirely too quickly for comfort. Fallen logs and sharp tree roots threatened to knock holes in the bottom of the vessels; they did eventually destroy the small supply boat. The men steered their remaining boat around the obstacles as well as they could. Still, it was a wild ride.

For a week, the river flowed almost due west. All at once, though, it began to twist sharply to the south. Sturt anticipated that the new direction signaled more changes ahead, and he was right. Before long, the explorers found themselves being swept out into another river, this one joining them from the east. Though Sturt could not have known it, it was the Murray—the more southerly of the two rivers Hume and Hovell had passed on their journey to the southern coast.

The complicated system of rivers, lakes, and bays in southeastern Australia intrigued European explorers for many years.

Sturt and the Aborigines

On his way down the Murrumbidgee and the Murray, Charles Sturt and his companions nearly lost their lives at the hands of a group of aborigines. The Australian natives had always had an uneasy relationship with European explorers, a relationship that dated back to the scuffle between the native peoples of the north coast and Willem Jansz's crew, during which one of the Dutch sailors had died. On their way down the Murrumbidgee, Sturt's party had met few aborigines, and those they had encountered had been reasonably friendly. But that soon changed.

Soon after the explorers entered the Murray, they encountered a large band of spear-carrying aborigines, who blocked their path. "A dead silence prevailed among those in the front ranks," Sturt wrote later, quoted in Roderick Cameron's *Australia: History and Horizons,* "but those in the background, as well as the women, who carried supplies of darts . . . were extremely clamorous." The current sped the travelers by the group, but the aborigines followed, shouting and gesturing angrily with their spears.

The travelers might not have survived, but all at once another group of aborigines appeared on the river's opposite bank. For reasons Sturt never fully understood, their leader immediately swam across the river to argue with the leader of the first band. As Sturt described it, as quoted in Cameron's book, the newcomer was "stamping with passion on the sand." Later anthropologists theorized that the second group mistook the Europeans for legendary heroes, but no one can say for certain what prompted such support. In any case, the first group gave in to the pleadings of the newcomer, and the travelers continued down the Murray unimpeded.

Aborigines (pictured) came into contact with several European expeditions through the Australian interior.

The Great River System

The Murray was much wider and gentler than the Murrumbidgee had been. Now the travelers moved along at a less frenetic pace—a pleasant change from the raging currents of the river where they had started their journey. Here, too, the scenery was nothing short of gorgeous, and Sturt was careful to note his observations whenever time permitted. His descriptions are considered among the most evocative of all explorers. "The cliffs under which we passed towered above us," he wrote at one point, "and the water dashed against their base like the waves of the sea."[51]

For the next week or so, the men continued west along the Murray. After a time, another river flowed in from the northeast to join them. Sturt decided to investigate. Pointing the boat into the current of this new tributary, he and his men rowed upstream for several miles. Sturt theorized that this was the Darling, the river he had sighted the previous year miles to the north of this part of the continent. And as it turned out, he was right. It was now clear that the great rivers of Australia's southeast were all part of the same network, or system. But the puzzle of where they ultimately led remained unsolved.

Sturt and his men now resumed their trek down the Murray, charting the twists and turns of the mighty river as best they could. For about two hundred miles, they continued to head west. Then their course abruptly turned south for two hundred miles more. Still the men headed on. At last, thirty-three days after leaving their base camp on the Murrumbidgee, the travelers arrived at the end of the river.

The sight, however, must have been somewhat disappointing. The Murray flowed into a series of small lakes just north of Australia's southern coast. From the ocean itself, there was scarcely a sign of the great river system that drained virtually the entire southeastern portion of the continent. Indeed, Matthew Flinders had sailed by the mouth of the Murray without noticing it at all. And no wonder: There was no great gap in the rocky shoreline, no powerful waterway churning out into the sea—just a small channel curving past a sandbar or two, a meek ending to a great network of rivers.

Now, Sturt was faced with a dilemma. He and his men were many hundreds of miles from New South Wales. Their boat could not travel that distance along the coastline. Sturt had hopes that a ship might happen by to return them to civilization, but he did not dare wait; the travelers were already low on supplies, and the nearby coastline had little food or water to offer.

On the other hand, the only alternative was a grueling journey up the rivers back to their base camp. It had taken thirty-three days to get this far; it seemed likely to take them longer to row back upstream, especially once they got into the wild currents of the Murrumbidgee. And the men had only about a month's worth of supplies remaining. Time was of the essence, and the margin for error was slim.

The men, however, had no choice but to try. At first, they made excellent progress

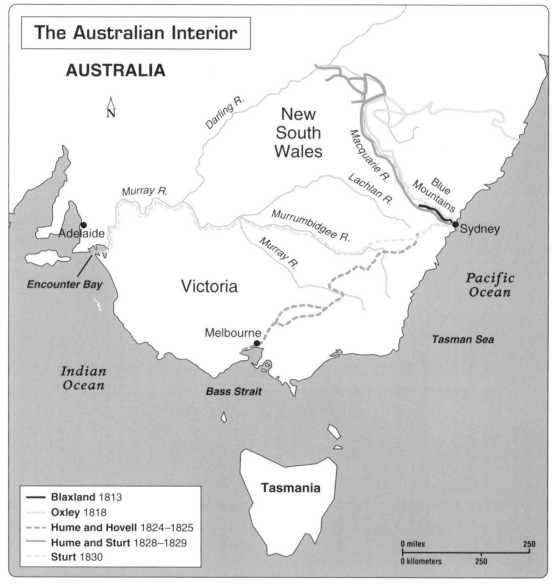

The Australian Interior

AUSTRALIA

N

Darling R.

New South Wales

Murray R.

Macquarie R.

Lachlan R.

Blue Mountains

Murrumbidgee R.

Adelaide

Sydney

Encounter Bay

Murray R.

Victoria

Pacific Ocean

Melbourne

Tasman Sea

Indian Ocean

Bass Strait

Tasmania

—— **Blaxland** 1813
—— **Oxley** 1818
‑ ‑ ‑ **Hume and Hovell** 1824–1825
—— **Hume and Sturt** 1828–1829
‑ ‑ ‑ **Sturt** 1830

0 miles   250
0 kilometers   250

navigating the six hundred or so miles of the Murray to its junction with the Murrumbidgee. But the second part of the trip was much harder. Weakened by nearly two months of steady travel, they found it extremely difficult to make any headway at all against the flooded Murrumbidgee. Nevertheless, they per-

sisted, even as their supplies ran lower and lower. Despite working on low rations and little rest, they made it back to base camp in just thirty days—three days less than the voyage downstream had taken.

But they were not yet safe. Base camp was empty. After two months of waiting

Australia's Natural History

The explorations of Australia were valuable not only for the geographical information they provided, but also for the unusual natural history they discovered. Isolated from the rest of the world for thousands of years, life developed in different ways on Australia than it did on other continents. The early explorers were deeply intrigued by such animals as kangaroos, wombats, koalas, and duck-billed platypuses, none of them known anywhere other than Australia.

The kangaroo in particular excited their imaginations. The Dutch captain François Pelsaert thought the animal was a kind of cat. James Cook disagreed, calling it "an animal something less than a greyhound, of a mouse colour, very slender made and swift of foot," as quoted in Roderick Cameron's book *Australia: History and Horizons*. Cook's naturalist, Joseph Banks, admitted that he was stumped as to how to classify the beast: "Nothing certainly that I have seen before resembles him." By 1790, in fact, a live kangaroo had been brought to England, where it was exhibited—and proved to be a tremendous attraction.

Trees and other plants, too, were different in Australia than elsewhere—even different from their counterparts in Indonesia and in the Pacific Islands. Gum trees and eucalyptus were everywhere, with occasional cedars and other species growing throughout the land. "The extreme uniformity of the vegetation is the most remarkable feature of the landscape," wrote the great biologist Charles Darwin upon visiting Australia in 1836, quoted in Cameron's *Australia: History and Horizons*. "The trees nearly all belong to one family, and mostly have their leaves in a vertical, instead of, as in Europe, a nearly horizontal position."

The koala, a marsupial endemic and unique to Australia, was first seen by Europeans in 1798 as they investigated the Blue Mountains.

for the travelers to return, the other members of the expedition had given up and left the area. There was no alternative but for the weary men to continue rowing up the Murrumbidgee. For the next three weeks Sturt and his companions pushed themselves to the limits of their endurance—and sometimes beyond. Sturt went temporarily blind. One of his companions went insane. Still, the men continued to battle the current, and despite everything, they made progress.

At last, however, the travelers could row no more. Sturt ordered a halt. He had the men set up a temporary camp, and ordered the two who were in the best physical condition to go in search of food and help. They returned several days later with both. The men struggled back to the inhabited sections of New South Wales, their ordeal finally over. Sturt and most of the others had been near death, but in the end, all the members of the expedition had survived.

Despite the hardships, though, Sturt's expedition had been tremendously successful. As Flinders had put to rest any serious doubt that Australia was a continent, so too had Sturt settled the question of the rivers of southeastern Australia. As Flinders had charted and described the coastline in detail, so had Sturt mapped and described the unknown lands west of the growing British colony. Flinders, Sturt, Hume, and others of this period had done excellent work filling in some of the blanks on the map of Australia. Unfortunately, the next set of blanks would prove far more difficult to fill than any other land anywhere in Australia or the Pacific.

CHAPTER FIVE

The Australian Outback

Sturt's expedition down the Murray was followed by several other expeditions that further investigated the great rivers of New South Wales. Between them, these explorers did important work in mapping the Darling, the Lachlan, and several other rivers. They found evidence to prove Sturt's theory that the rivers all formed a single network, and they helped open parts of the region to further European settlement. Increasingly, though, the attention of adventurous Australians was drawn not to the temperate southeastern section of their continent, but toward the great unknown interior instead.

The Australian interior, sometimes called the Outback, was a mystery indeed. Thanks to Flinders and a few others, the continental coastline was reasonably well-known. But except in the southeast, no European knew what lay inside that boundary. Flinders had encountered no major rivers in his survey of the coast, a fact that suggested a dry interior, and of course the mariners who had sailed along the northern and western shores of Aus-

tralia had noted the dryness as well. "Barren it must be called," a member of James Cook's crew had written, "and in a very high degree."[52]

Still, there was no guarantee that the interior of Australia was as dry as the observations of Flinders, Cook, and others indicated. The land was huge, with plenty of space for mountain ranges, fertile prairies, even inland seas such as Sturt and Oxley had imagined might lie in the southeast. A few people believed that there might even be a lost civilization somewhere in the center of the continent.

Beginning in 1840, a series of explorers determined to find out the truth. One by one, they ventured into the heart of the Outback, chipping slowly away at the unknown spaces on the map of Australia. The task was monumental. The Australian interior proved harsh and unforgiving, robbing even the most confident and physically fit adventurers of their health and sometimes their lives. "Exploration of a thousand miles in Australia," wrote one veteran explorer, "is equal to ten thousand miles in any other part of

Hardy explorers traversing the Australian Outback found it to be an extremely dry and barren landscape.

the earth's surface, always excepting Arctic and Antarctic travel."[53]

Still, the adventurers who visited the Outback did their best to conquer the land. They cut through swamps, clambered across rocks, and coped with brutal heat. They traveled along Australia's southern coast and cut through the extreme northern territories. Through it all, they kept an ultimate goal in mind: to achieve the grand prize of Australian exploration by becoming the first to cross the entire Australian continent from south to north.

Edward Eyre

Among the first explorers to venture into the Outback was a farmer named Edward Eyre. An adventurer at heart, Eyre first tried to penetrate the interior on horseback in 1839. He began by heading directly north from the new settlement of Adelaide, near the mouth of the Murray on Australia's southern coast. For a time the journey took him and his companions through forested land similar to that through which Sturt had traveled.

But as Eyre continued north, the scenery shifted dramatically. The land dried out, trees became scarce, and an apparently infinite landscape of sand and rock stretched in front of him. After a few hundred miles of harsh, dry terrain, Eyre came upon a largely dry lake bed filled with mud and topped with a crust of salt. He tried to push through the salty muck, but the horses' hooves sank through the crusty covering with every step they took. When the horses had sunk into the ooze nearly to the tops of their saddles, Eyre turned back, resolving, as he put it, to "waste no more time or energy on so desolate and forbidding a region."[54]

But though Eyre had no further interest in the area around this lake bed—now called Lake Eyre in his honor—he soon had another expedition in mind. The Australian economy, he knew, relied heavily on livestock, particularly sheep. It would be useful to have an overland route along which to take livestock from the southeastern part of the continent to several new settlements on the south-

western shore. Accordingly, Eyre set out to determine if such a route was feasible.

Technically, Eyre was not planning to enter the Australian interior. Leaving in early 1841 from Port Lincoln, west of Adelaide and about a thousand miles from the continent's western boundary, he planned instead to follow the southern coast of the continent as far as practicable. Still, his journey would take him through territory every bit as inhospitable as any point in the center of Australia. "It

Edward Eyre first attempted to penetrate the harsh Outback region in 1839.

is the loneliest region imaginable," writes historian Alan Moorehead. "Even today no man in his right senses would attempt to make this journey on foot."[55] According to Moorehead, even the aborigines stayed away from the area—and with good reason, as Eyre was soon to discover.

"Suffering and Distress"

Eyre started with a party of nine, but soon sent back all but his farm manager, James Baxter, and three aborigines. The journey was brutal. The sun beat down upon the travelers, and horseflies pestered them constantly. The terrain was harsh and rocky, the winds strong and relentless. Worst of all, though, was the sand. "Our provisions were smothered with it," Eyre wrote, "and our blankets half buried when we lay down at nights—it was a perpetual and never-ceasing torment."[56]

The problems of Eyre and his companions, however, went beyond flies, winds, and an excess of sand. The real issue was water. The land was unimaginably dry. With virtually no surface water anywhere, the travelers had to dig into the earth in search of underground pools, which were tiny at best and filled with salt water at worst. At one point, the horses went for five days without drinking; at another, the men used a sponge to collect traces of dew to slake their thirst.

The situation was so bad, in fact, that two of the aborigines eventually ran off, taking most of the expedition's food supply with them. When Baxter tried to stop them, they seized the group's best rifle and shot him dead. Eyre half wished he had been the one to be killed: "Suffering and distress had well-nigh overwhelmed me," he wrote in his diary, "and life hardly seemed worth the effort to prolong it."[57] Yet in the end, he had no choice but to continue, along with the remaining aborigine, Wylie.

After several weeks on the move, Eyre and Wylie at last moved into gentler territory. The land was dotted here and there with watering holes, and the winter rainy season was beginning. Still, the two explorers were in very poor physical shape, and there was no guarantee that they would ever arrive at King George Sound, their destination. But just when conditions seemed to be at their bleakest, the men's circumstances changed—and in a way, Eyre wrote, "so great, so sudden, and so unexpected it seemed more like a dream than reality."[58]

On June 2, while still several hundred miles from the western coast, the two men unexpectedly sighted a whaling ship on the horizon. Eyre lit a fire to attract the crew's attention, and a small boat came to the coast to ferry the travelers out to the ship. For nearly two weeks, the travelers enjoyed the hospitality of the ship's captain, who fed them, gave them new clothes, and let them rest aboard the ship. The captain would have taken them to King George Sound, too, but Eyre politely refused. Refreshed and provisioned for the final miles, Eyre and Wylie finished the trip—on foot—in early July.

Steep dunes, windswept sands, and dry conditions presented a major problem for Outback explorers like Eyre.

The pair's experience had demonstrated that travel in the Outback was grueling and dangerous. But Eyre and Wylie had also proved that travel across the rugged and unyielding terrain of Australia was possible. Future explorers would recognize the men's difficulties—but would pay far closer attention to their ultimate success.

Sturt's Next Journey

The next important expedition to venture into the Outback was led by a familiar name—Charles Sturt, the man who had voyaged down the Murrumbidgee and Murray rivers. Despite his discoveries in the southeast, Sturt still suspected that an inland sea lurked somewhere in the center of the continent. His expedition,

Food and Water

All of the European explorers who investigated Australia's interior were courageous and resourceful, and most were skilled in survival techniques. Yet one thread stands out in their stories: a consistent inability to live off the land when supplies ran low.

To a great extent, the reason lay in the terrain. The Australian Outback is indeed an inhospitable place, with few natural food supplies and very little water. Yet at the same time, difficult conditions are not a complete explanation of the explorers' difficulties. The aborigines, after all, had lived in the harsh climate of the region for thousands of years. Clearly, the terrain played a part—but only a part—in the explorers' inability to find food and water.

The rest probably involved experience. Even veteran explorers of European background knew little about Australia in comparison to the aborigines. The Europeans lacked the huge storehouse of knowledge that came from generations of living in the region. They did not know the best ways of hunting and trapping Australian animals or even which animals would make the best eating; they were not aware of all the systems the aborigines used to get and preserve water in times of drought. And they had no idea of the nutritional value of some of the grains growing on the continent. Most English explorers of the period, whether in Africa, the Arctic, or Australia, did not bother to learn from the natives, and, as the case of Australia suggests, the results were sometimes tragic.

though, was less about proving his point than it was about knowledge, adventure, and glory. "Let any man lay the map of Australia before him, and regard the blank upon its surface," he wrote, "and then let me ask him if it would not be an honourable achievement to be the first to place foot in its centre."[59]

Sturt was a veteran explorer, experienced in wilderness survival. In this case, though, his judgment was perhaps clouded by the prospect of glory. Despite Eyre's reports that the area north of Adelaide lacked freshwater, Sturt put together a large expedition that included not only sixteen men but also about 250 animals, mostly sheep, both for carrying

supplies and to use as food. The travelers also brought along a boat, although there was no guarantee that they would find navigable water—or any water at all, for that matter.

In late 1844, Sturt began his expedition from Adelaide. He headed more or less northeast, staying as close as he could to the forested southeastern section of the continent. Before long, though, he emerged onto the flat plains of the Australian interior. Although the country was rapidly growing drier and more difficult, Sturt commanded the men to keep going. By January 1845, the height of the Australian summer, they were in a region of dunes and salt flats no more welcoming than any of the territories through which Edward Eyre had passed.

Now, Sturt and his men were in trouble. The summer of 1844 to 1845 was one of the hottest and driest on record in Australia. As daytime temperatures routinely climbed to 120 degrees Fahrenheit, the few remaining waterholes dried up. To turn back was impossible, and Sturt recognized that he had erred. "We were locked up in the desolated and heated region," he wrote, "as effectually as if we had wintered at the Pole." [60] The only chance was to find the largest remaining source of water in the area—and then hold out until cooler, wetter weather arrived.

"The Stillness of Death"

The men soon found a single pond that had not totally vanished in the heat. Digging themselves an underground room to avoid the heat of the sun, they waited as the waters slowly diminished. The nine feet of water in the pond when the men arrived dwindled agonizingly to five feet, then three, then two. "The stillness of death reigned around us," Sturt wrote. "No living creature was to be heard; nothing visible inhabited that dreary desert but the ant, even the fly shunned it." [61]

The rains eventually did come, in July, and just in time. The six-month ordeal had killed one man and demoralized the rest. Astonishingly, though, Sturt refused to return to Adelaide. Instead, he and some of his men resumed their trek into the continent while the others—no doubt

gratefully—headed home. Before long the remaining men came to another broad plain with very little water. Unknown to Sturt, this was a section of the Australian desert where rain scarcely ever falls. Farther south, he had encountered a dry summer and a wet winter; here, it was dry all the time.

Still, the men stumbled forward. Their feet were burned by superheated sand and cut by sharp rocks. Their tongues swelled from lack of water. In early November, the travelers reached another oasis, which Sturt called Cooper's Creek (today most commonly known as Cooper Creek). Here, reluctantly, Sturt finally ordered the men to turn around. Even so, they barely made it home; Sturt himself collapsed on the return trip, a victim of poor nutrition, dehydration, and most of all, exhaustion. Finding the center of Australia, he had once said, was "an object worthy to perish one's life for." [62] He had nearly done exactly that.

The Race Begins

For the twelve years following Sturt's return from the desert, exploration largely ignored Australia's middle. A succession of expeditions focused instead on investigating the fringes of the Outback. Thomas Mitchell made a survey of the northeastern corner of the continent. Ludwig Leichhardt made a trek across northern Australia. Augustus Gregory pioneered a new path between Adelaide and a region north of Cooper's Creek and made another expedition paralleling Leichhardt's route. Each expedition revealed important information about Australian geography.

But each expedition also pointed out, once again, the hardships and dangers of travel in Australia's interior. The northern coast of the continent proved to be choked with muddy marshes, so thick in places as to be almost impenetrable. Elsewhere, water was virtually impossible to find; rivers dried up in the summer heat or divided into tiny creeks that quickly burrowed into the ground. "Not one single stream emanates from this inhospitable region,"[63] lamented Gregory about the land north of Cooper's Creek. And Leichhardt and his companions paid the ultimate price: After marching off into the Outback for a second expedition in 1848, they were never seen again.

If explorers of the time were eager to avoid the intolerable conditions of Australia's center, though, government offi-

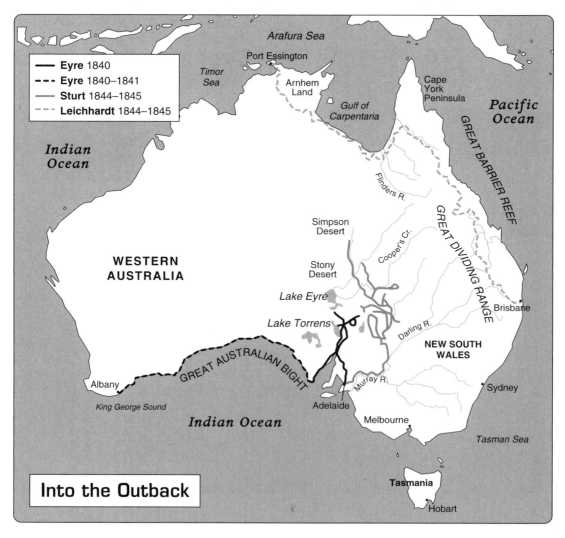

Into the Outback

The British colony at Melbourne arose during Australia's settlement boom of the mid-1800s.

cials had a different agenda. By the 1850s, Australia was growing rapidly. No longer confined to present-day New South Wales in the southeast, major settlements were springing up along other sections of the coasts: Adelaide and Melbourne along the southern coast, Brisbane in the northeast, Albany in the southwest. It seemed important to link these distant towns with the new invention of the telegraph—and, eventually, to extend the telegraph lines to Asia and ultimately to Europe as well.

To find the best routes for these telegraph lines across Australia's interior, further exploration was essential. Under ideal circumstances, the territories that made up the Australian colony would have cooperated in choosing an explorer and directing him on a possible path across the continent. But by the late 1850s, the rivalry between Adelaide and Melbourne had grown too intense for cooperation. The people of Melbourne, in particular, wanted to prove that any line across the continent should travel north from their city.

And so the leaders of Melbourne set up their own expedition. Financed by business leaders, ordinary citizens, and the territorial government itself, this expedition was to leave from Melbourne and make its way to the northern coast of the continent. Then the explorers would turn around and return home, having demonstrated—or so the expedition's backers hoped—that the route from Melbourne was the ideal place to set up Australia's telegraph line. The plan was far-reaching and grandiose, and its backers were supremely confident. There was only one problem: the expedition's leader.

Burke Sets Out

The man chosen to lead the expedition was Robert Burke. Born in Ireland in 1820, Burke had come to Australia in 1853 and taken a job on the police force. All who knew him recognized that he was dashing, courageous, energetic, and strong. Moreover, as a contemporary put it, Burke was a "well-bred gentleman . . . quite at home amongst people of the best class,"[64] which automatically qualified him for a leadership position in the eyes of many Australians. The committee charged with selecting a leader had few doubts; they picked Burke by a solid majority over two other strong candidates.

Burke had character, and he had ancestry. What he lacked was exploring experience. He had never been on any significant expedition; nor, for that matter, had he spent any time in the Australian Outback. His knowledge of wilderness survival was sketchy, his ability to determine latitude and longitude was nonexistent, and his sense of direction was notoriously bad. "He could not tell the north from the south in broad daylight,"[65] one journalist complained. Yet the committee had made its choice.

In August 1860, the expedition set out from Melbourne, with Burke at the head of a column of nineteen men, six wagons, and almost fifty camels and horses. Burke had imagined that the expedition would move along quickly, but in fact the travelers moved forward with agonizing slowness. The wagons were difficult to maneuver; the animals needed time to graze. Worse, Burke was disorganized, slapdash, and inclined to take unnecessary risks—so much so that several of the group's most experienced members quit in disgust. "Camping places were not selected until after dark," wrote one observer. "At every camp, lots of tools, axes and spades were left."[66]

After two months, the travelers had gone only about five hundred miles. At this point, Burke tired of the slow progress. Hoping to hurry things up, he divided the group in two. Then he led half of the men to Cooper's Creek, the northernmost point reached by Sturt, taking with him only the bare minimum of supplies. The trip was smooth, one of Burke's men even describing the journey as "a picnic party."[67] The remaining equipment was to follow with the rest of the men. Once the second group reached Cooper's Creek, Burke planned to push north toward Australia's northern boundary.

But as time passed and the second group did not arrive at Cooper's Creek, Burke grew impatient. By mid-December, four months after leaving Melbourne, he decided he could wait no longer. Leaving his assistant William Brahe and several other men to wait for the rear party, Burke headed north into the desert with three members of the expedition: William Wills, John King, and Charles Gray. The men took a few camels, one horse, and enough food for ninety days.

Robert Burke set off from Melbourne in 1860 to help find a workable route for a north-south telegraph line across Australia.

To the Swamps

Burke assumed that ninety days would be all his group would need. And at first, the men seemed to be making good time. But they had set themselves a difficult task. The northern ocean lay about a thousand miles away, across territory that was almost entirely unexplored. Whatever supplies the men carried would have to get them to the northern coast—and back to Cooper's Creek. To be sure of surviving the return journey, the men would need to reach their destination by late January, six weeks after leaving their depot.

Traveling conditions were in their favor. Much of the terrain was fairly smooth, and water proved to be less a problem than the men had feared. They found a river in early January and followed it much of the way toward the coast. Occasionally, they traveled forty miles or more in a single day. Still, the end of January found them about 150 miles from the coast.

Burke never hesitated. He ordered his group to press on, and press on they did. As they ventured farther north, they found the desert rapidly giving way to tropical swamps and thickets. Moving forward through the mud and the tangles became more and more difficult and finally became practically impossible. The men knew they were close to the coast—the swamp water was salty and rose and fell with the tides—but they could not find a passage through the marshes. In mid-February, they gave up the attempt. "It would be well to say that we reached the sea," wrote Burke in his

Camels in the Outback

Burke's expedition was not the only Australian adventure to make use of camels. In fact, camels were an obvious solution to the problem of crossing the great Australian deserts. Native to the deserts of the Middle East and Asia, camels can go for long periods of time without a drink; they are strong, too, and can carry much heavier loads, pound for pound, than any horse. "What might not be expected from an exploring party equipped with these ships of the desert?" asked an Australian newspaper, quoted in Sarah Murgatroyd's *The Dig Tree*.

Camels certainly did have their uses. On expeditions into the desert, they proved quite valuable. They were content with almost any kind of food, and their narrow ears and long eyelashes helped make them impervious to sand. Likewise, their ability to remain hydrated without freshwater came in handy, as long as there was a source of freshwater a few days' journey ahead.

But the camels were not as effective as some Australians believed. Their hooves, well adapted to sand, were not used to rocks and pebbles such as littered parts of the Australian deserts; walking through these regions slowed the animals considerably and sometimes injured their feet. Camels are known as bad-tempered creatures, too, which precluded companionship such as many explorers of the past have gotten from their horses. And while the camels were indeed strong, they were not built to carry freight. Packs slipped down their humps, causing abscesses and abrasions. Part of Burke's problem was an overestimate of what camels could actually do.

Camels carry European explorers through the inhospitable Australian Outback.

diary, "but we could not obtain a view of the open ocean."[68]

They had come as close as they could, however, and it was time to retrace their steps. The journey north from Cooper's Creek should have taken six weeks; instead, it had taken two months. One month's supply of food remained for the return journey. Now, they were racing against time.

The Return Trip

Burke and his companions hurried south as quickly as they could. Finding their way was not an issue, but making good time proved difficult. Now, conditions were appalling. It rained continually for the first two or three weeks, and the landscape became a sea of mud. "The ground so boggy as to be almost impassable,"[69] the usually optimistic Wills complained one day in his diary.

Worse, the men were growing weak and weary. In an attempt to stretch what little food they carried, Burke had ordered the travelers' rations cut in half. Unfortunately, the men were already in poor physical condition from having been on the move for several months, and the reduced food supplies quickly made matters a good deal worse. Despite their need to set a quick pace, the men were having increasing difficulty making any progress at all. By March 7, three weeks after they had turned around, they had traveled barely a hundred miles. Not until March 25, three weeks later, did they finally reach the halfway point between the northern coast and Cooper's Creek.

But by this time, the travelers were in desperate shape. Knowing their lives depended on speed, they jettisoned dozens of pounds of equipment—books, ropes,

Burke (middle) and two of his men approach Cooper's Creek on their return trip to Melbourne.

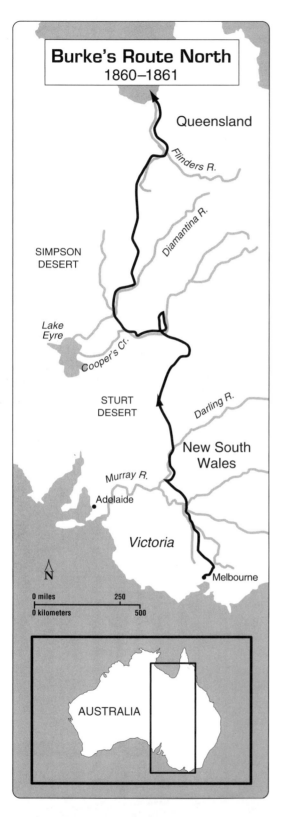

Burke's Route North
1860–1861

Queensland

Flinders R.

Diamantina R.

SIMPSON DESERT

Lake Eyre

Cooper's Cr.

STURT DESERT

Darling R.

New South Wales

Murray R.

Adelaide

Victoria

N

Melbourne

0 miles 250
0 kilometers 500

AUSTRALIA

surveying tools. They gathered small plants to supplement their meager diet; at one point, they killed and ate a python. They butchered two camels and their horse, eating what meat remained on their bones. Tired, hungry, and increasingly unwell, the explorers continued to drag themselves south. It was truly a race for survival.

On April 17, Charles Gray collapsed into delirium and died. Exhausted as they were, his companions spent the day burying him; then, they resumed the trek. Despite all their hardships, they knew they were only a few days' march from Cooper's Creek and the supply depot. Indeed, just four days later, they marshaled all their remaining strength and made the final push into the camp. "I think I see their tents ahead," Burke said again and again as they neared the supply depot. "I think I see them."[70]

But he did not. The depot was deserted. The rear party, with the bulk of the expedition's supplies, had never arrived. Brahe had waited as long as he dared for Burke to return, but he did not have the resources to wait indefinitely. Burke had planned to return a month earlier, and Brahe could wait no longer. He had packed up and left—and in terrible timing, he had departed the morning of the very day Burke, Wills, and King finally arrived.

Aftermath

Burke and his men were bitterly distressed at the news. Instead of following Brahe,

John McDouall Stuart

Robert Burke's need for haste may have been partly a character trait and partly a reflection of his lack of experience as an explorer. But it was also motivated by fear of competition. Although Burke had been given plenty of money and attention, he was not the only man attempting to make the south-to-north crossing of Australia. Another adventurer, John McDouall Stuart, was doing the same.

Unlike Burke, Stuart was a veteran explorer. He had been a member of Sturt's earlier expedition to Cooper's Creek, and he had made several valuable discoveries of his own in the deserts north of Adelaide. Unlike Burke, too, he knew when to give up. In early 1860, preceding Burke's attempt, Stuart set out from Adelaide to make a south-north crossing of the continent. He and his companions reached a point he called Attack Creek, well north of the center of Australia, though many miles west of where Burke would travel. But there, a few hundred miles short of the northern coast, Stuart realized that his supplies were running low. Rather than push forward and risk his life, Stuart opted to return home.

Stuart would try twice more. In 1861, he retraced his steps to Attack Creek and tried to find a safe route north. Forced to give up by the thick tangled underbrush of tropical Australia, he returned home once again. Later that year, just after rescuers found John King, Stuart gave it one more try. This time he found a path north of Attack Creek and followed a plain to the sea. Wading in, he set up a British flag and added, as quoted in Ian Mudie's *The Heroic Journey of John McDouall Stuart*, "I have tried all my life to do this, and have now succeeded."

the travelers decided to head in a different direction, across the Outback to a police station they thought was about 150 miles away. The support party had left behind some rations should the travelers appear, and the food did help revive the men—but only a little. "We are very weak," wrote Burke in a note he left at Cooper's Creek. "We shall not be able to travel faster than four or five miles a day."[71]

He was right. By May 8, they had traveled about fifty miles, but their remaining camels had died. Weary as they were, the men found it impossible to venture farther without the help of the animals.

For a time, friendly aborigines kept them alive by providing them with fish, rats, and a kind of grass seed called *nardoo*. When the aborigines moved on, the explorers stayed behind and did their best to find food on their own. By late June, hunger and illness had taken their course. "I may live four or five days if the weather continues warm," Wills wrote in his journal. "My legs and arms are nearly skin and bones."[72] Burke was scarcely any better off. By early July, both Wills and Burke were dead.

Only the fourth member of the party, John King, would survive the ordeal, and he would do so only through the concerted efforts of the aborigines. A group of natives fed him and helped him build a shelter. "They treated me with uniform kindness," King would report later, "and looked upon me as one of themselves."[73] In mid-September, a rescue party arrived in the area in search of the missing explorers. As rescuer Edwin Welch rode along a small creek, he noticed a skinny figure standing in a clearing. Looking closely, Welch recognized that this person was no aborigine. "What in the name of wonder are you?" he demanded. "The last man of the Exploring Expedition,"[74] King replied, and then burst into tears.

The Last Blanks

In the end, Burke's expedition had been a tragedy. The expedition had been too large and slow-moving, and Burke's leadership had been questionable at best. At the very least, he should have turned around in late January, if not earlier, instead of marching all the way to the tidal marshes of the northern coast. His insistence on pushing forward, combined with impatience, disorganization, and plain bad luck, all helped contribute to his own death and those of two of his followers.

Yet from an explorer's perspective, Burke and his men had achieved much. They had penetrated the unknown lands north of Cooper's Creek, charted many natural features, and cast further doubt on the idea of a great inland sea. Wills had made many records of the area's plant and animal life. Most of all, they had proved that a south-to-north crossing of the Australian Outback was indeed possible. Building on the work of Eyre and Sturt, Burke and his men had filled in some of the largest blanks on the map of Australia.

However, the greatest strides in filling the blanks came not because of Burke's efforts so much as because of his death. After Burke and his men were deemed to be lost, five different rescue expeditions set out to look for the travelers. Between them, they journeyed more than eight thousand miles in search of the missing men. While some of this travel took the rescuers through country that had already been explored, much more did not. By the time the rescue teams had all returned home—remarkably, without a single loss of life—virtually the entire eastern half of Australia was known to Europeans, and the western half would soon follow. The great Australian Outback, at last, was no longer a mystery.

Exploration and Exploitation

By 1880, most of Australia, like nearly all of the Pacific Islands, had been visited, explored, and charted by Europeans. Oceania, once so removed and so isolated from the rest of humanity, was no longer unknown. And while the physical distances between these places and the great population centers of Asia, Europe, or the Americas remained enormous, in another sense the distances had shrunk considerably.

Suddenly in some cases, gradually in others, the Pacific islands and Australia were losing their remoteness. In 1872 a telegraph line was strung up across Australia, following the route north from Adelaide, and linked to one originating in Asia. Several Pacific Islands were pressed into service as military bases by the United States, England, and other nations, with regular arrivals by naval vessels and sailors. Whaleships from New England landed in the harbors of Tahiti and Fiji to replenish their supplies. Emigrants from Britain set up sheep farms and towns in Australia and New Zealand; Christian missionaries flocked to the Pacific in hopes of converting the islanders to Christianity.

In some ways, the effects of these newcomers were positive. Doctors and other trained medical personnel built hospitals where there had previously been none. The introduction of metals to the Pacific Islands certainly improved the quality of life among the people of the region; newer technologies, ranging from cars to the Internet, continue to do the same today.

In other ways, however, the influx of the outside world has been catastrophic for the native societies of Australia and the Pacific Islands. Through time, newcomers, usually well armed, have muscled their way into the lightly populated regions of the Pacific, pushing aside the local populations and seizing land and resources for themselves. Native culture has suffered as well. Many people of the Pacific discarded their traditional beliefs in favor of the Christian ideals preached by the missionaries. In the wake of the newcomers, indeed, many peoples of the region have gradually lost their

A Catholic missionary and four aborigine boys pose at an Australian mission. Many missionaries flocked to Australia and the Pacific Islands hoping to convert the natives to Christianity.

cultures, their identities, and even their lives.

Modern Problems

Sometimes, the native populations have simply been pushed aside by newcomers, who quickly come to make up a new majority. In Hawaii, for instance, the dominant ethnic groups today are white and Asian; no more than one Hawaiian in five is descended in any way from the people who lived on the islands when Cook arrived, and only about one of every hundred is a full-blooded ethnic Hawaiian. New Zealand, similarly, is dominated not by Maoris but by white New Zealanders, most of them of British origin. The cultures of Hawaii and New Zealand today bear very little resemblance to traditional island society.

Even where native islanders remain a majority, European visitors have caused great changes to life and culture. Tahiti, for example, is part of French Polynesia, a territory that belongs to France despite the overwhelming Polynesian majority in the area. For years, France took steps to discourage Tahitian culture, at one point banning native languages in the schools. Economically, too, France eliminated Tahiti's traditional self-sufficiency and made the territory dependent on France for food and other materials. And for thirty years beginning in 1966, the French government used its Polynesian possessions as test sites for nuclear weapons—with predictable consequences for the environment as well as on the health of the people.

And in some cases, the ultimate effect of the explorers has been particularly stark. That has been especially true in Australia. Native Tasmanians—the people heard, but not seen, by Abel Tasman—were practically wiped out in the 1800s, the victims of disease and oppression by European settlers; today, traditional Tasmanian culture is long dead. The aborigines of the mainland, in turn, have been the victims of extreme racial prejudice—much of it perfectly legal until quite recently. Even today, most Australian aborigines live in poverty, their social structure and cultural ways badly disrupted.

It is entirely fair to associate these changes, positive and negative, with the early explorers to the area. Through their voyages, men such as Mendaña, Tasman, Wallis, and Sturt brought the people of Australia and the Pacific into contact with the outside world. Some of these explorers, such as Cook and Flinders, had rela-

tively benign influences on the people they encountered. But most early European adventurers treated the natives with suspicion at best and with hostility at worst. To them, the people of the Pacific were not fellow humans so much as obstacles to be conquered. Their attitudes and actions set the tone for what was to follow.

France began conducting nuclear bomb tests on islands in French Polynesia starting in 1966.

Legacy

Nevertheless, the legacy of the early European explorers goes well beyond their treatment of the Pacific peoples. The fact remains that the men who investigated Australia and the Pacific Islands were among the bravest and most remarkable of all explorers. From Magellan to the men who searched for Burke, these adventurers gathered knowledge on thousands of square miles of unknown ocean, island, and continent, usually at great risk to themselves. They dealt with coral reefs, rode out storms, and survived endless stretches of empty ocean; they traversed mighty rivers, crossed barren deserts, and hacked their way through tidal swamps.

The achievements of these men were impressive indeed. They studied the plants, animals, and peoples of Australia and the Pacific; they recorded the ocean currents and the locations of mountains and rivers. They returned to Europe with charts showing islands that no European had ever seen and indicating deserts drier than any part of their own homelands. They surveyed the Australian interior, they charted miles of trackless sea, they marked the positions of hundreds of islands. Not all of these explorers found what they were looking for. But they jointly succeeded in adding immeasurably to human knowledge of the planet—and that, in the end, was perhaps all that mattered.

Notes

Introduction: Oceania and Its People

1. David Lewis, *The Voyaging Stars*. New York: W.W. Norton, 1978, p. 54.

Chapter One: Early European Visitors

2. Quoted in Antonio Pigafetta, *The First Voyage Around the World*. New York: Marsilio, 1995, p. 26.
3. Quoted in Pigafetta, *The First Voyage Around the World,* p. 27.
4. Quoted in Oliver E. Allen, *The Pacific Navigators*. Alexandria, VA: Time-Life, 1980, p. 17.
5. Quoted in Hakluyt Society, *The Discovery of the Solomon Islands*. London: Hakluyt Society, 1891, p. xxii.
6. Quoted in Hakluyt Society, *The Discovery of the Solomon Islands,* p. 40.
7. Quoted in Allen, *The Pacific Navigators,* p. 21.
8. Quoted in Hakluyt Society, *The Discovery of the Solomon Islands,* p. 135.
9. Quoted in Allen, *The Pacific Navigators,* p. 28.
10. Quoted in Allen, *The Pacific Navigators,* p. 30.
11. Quoted in Piers Pennington, *The Great Explorers*. New York: Facts On File, 1979, p. 239.

Chapter Two: Australia, the South Pacific, and the Dutch

12. Quoted in Andrew Sharp, *The Discovery of Australia*. Oxford, England: Clarendon Press, 1963, p. 19.
13. Quoted in Roderick Cameron, *Australia: History and Horizons*. New York: Columbia University Press, 1971, p. 23.
14. Quoted in Sharp, *The Discovery of Australia,* p. 42.
15. Quoted in Sharp, *The Discovery of Australia,* p. 62.
16. Quoted in Allen, *The Pacific Navigators,* p. 51.
17. Quoted in Allen, *The Pacific Navigators,* p. 53.
18. Quoted in Pennington, *The Great Explorers,* p. 248.
19. Quoted in Keith Sinclair, *A History of New Zealand*. London: Oxford University Press, 1961, p. 18.
20. Quoted in Sharp, *The Discovery of Australia,* p. 72.
21. Quoted in Cameron, *Australia,* p. 28.
22. Quoted in Sinclair, *A History of New Zealand,* p. 18.
23. Quoted in Allen, *The Pacific Navigators,* pp. 58–59.
24. Quoted in Pennington, *The Great Explorers,* p. 250.
25. Quoted in Allen, *The Pacific Navigators,* p. 62.

26. Quoted in Sinclair, *A History of New Zealand,* p. 18.

27. Quoted in Sharp, *The Discovery of Australia,* p. 87.

Chapter 3: Science and Romance

28. Quoted in George Robertson, *The Discovery of Tahiti.* London: Hakluyt Society, 1948, p. xxiii.

29. Quoted in Robertson, *The Discovery of Tahiti,* p. 103.

30. Quoted in Robertson, *The Discovery of Tahiti,* p. 135.

31. Quoted in David Howarth, *Tahiti: A Paradise Lost.* New York: Viking Press, 1983, p. 13.

32. Quoted in Allen, *The Pacific Navigators,* p. 89.

33. Quoted in Pennington, *The Great Explorers,* p. 254.

34. Quoted in Allen, *The Pacific Navigators,* p. 116.

35. Quoted in Cameron, *Australia,* p. 39.

36. Quoted in Pennington, *The Great Explorers,* p. 256.

37. Quoted in Roderick Cameron, *The Golden Haze.* Cleveland: World, 1964, p. 153.

38. Quoted in Allen, *The Pacific Navigators,* p. 152.

39. Johann Reinhold Forster, *The Resolution Journal of Johann Reinhold Forster.* London: Hakluyt Society, 1982, p. 651.

Chapter 4: Investigating Australia

40. Quoted in Pennington, *The Great Explorers,* p. 262.

41. Quoted in K.A. Austin, *The Voyage of the Investigator.* Adelaide, Australia: Rigby, 1964, p. 78.

42. Quoted in Austin, *The Voyage of the Investigator,* p. 89.

43. Quoted in Sharp, *The Discovery of Australia,* pp. 274–75.

44. Quoted in Pennington, *The Great Explorers,* p. 263.

45. Quoted in Cameron, *Australia,* p. 85.

46. Quoted in Pennington, *The Great Explorers,* p. 264.

47. Quoted in Cameron, *Australia,* p. 135.

48. Quoted in Pennington, *The Great Explorers,* p. 265.

49. Quoted in Pennington, *The Great Explorers,* p. 265.

50. Quoted in Cameron, *Australia,* p. 159.

51. Quoted in Cameron, *Australia,* p. 162.

Chapter 5: The Australian Outback

52. Quoted in Alan Moorehead, *The Fatal Impact.* New York: Harper and Row, 1966, p. 112.

53. Quoted in Cameron, *Australia,* p. 169.

54. Quoted in Alan Moorehead, *Cooper's Creek.* New York: Harper and Row, 1963, p. 14.

55. Moorehead, *The Fatal Impact,* pp. 155–56.

56. Quoted in Cameron, *Australia,* p. 167.

57. Quoted in Moorehead, *The Fatal Impact,* pp. 159–60.

58. Quoted in Moorehead, *The Fatal Impact,* p. 165.

59. Quoted in Sarah Murgatroyd, *The Dig Tree.* New York: Broadway, 2002, p. 1.

60. Quoted in Murgatroyd, *The Dig Tree,* pp. 10–11.

61. Quoted in Cameron, *Australia,* p. 170.
62. Quoted in Pennington, *The Great Explorers,* p. 266.
63. Quoted in Murgatroyd, *The Dig Tree,* p. 15.
64. Quoted in Moorehead, *Cooper's Creek,* p. 29.
65. Quoted in Murgatroyd, *The Dig Tree,* p. 62.
66. Quoted in Murgatroyd, *The Dig Tree,* p. 102.
67. Quoted in Moorehead, *Cooper's Creek,* p. 64.
68. Quoted in Murgatroyd, *The Dig Tree,* p. 202.
69. Quoted in Murgatroyd, *The Dig Tree,* p. 209.
70. Quoted in Moorehead, *Cooper's Creek,* p. 94.
71. Quoted in Pennington, *The Great Explorers,* pp. 270–71.
72. Quoted in Cameron, *Australia,* p. 178.
73. Quoted in Moorehead, *Cooper's Creek,* p. 148.
74. Quoted in Murgatroyd, *The Dig Tree,* p. 275.

Chronology

ca. 40,000 B.C.
Australian aborigines settle Australia.

ca. 3500 B.C.
Melanesians and Micronesians settle western Pacific Islands.

ca. 1500 B.C.
Polynesian settlement of Pacific Islands begins.

A.D. 1520
Ferdinand Magellan sails into Pacific through the Strait of Magellan.

1521
Magellan sails across the Pacific and visits Guam; Magellan is killed in the Philippines.

1568
Álvaro de Mendaña and Pedro Sarmiento visit the Solomon Islands.

1595
Mendaña visits the Marquesas and tries to colonize the Santa Cruz Islands.

1605
Pedro Fernandez de Quiros visits the Duff Islands and Vanuatu.

1606
Luis Torres sails through the Torres Strait north of Australia; Willem Jansz sails along the Cape York Peninsula.

1615
Willem Schouten and Jakob Le Maire reach Tuamotu and the Horn Islands.

1616
Dirck Hartog sights the west coast of Australia.

1627
François Thijssen sails along part of Australia's southern coast.

1629
François Pelsaert takes a small boat along Australia's west coast.

1642
Abel Tasman and Frans Visscher reach Tasmania and New Zealand.

1643
Tasman and Visscher visit Tonga.

1644
Tasman and Visscher trace the northern coast of Australia.

1721–1722
Jacob Roggeveen visits Easter Island, Samoa, and Tuamotu.

1767
Samuel Wallis visits Tahiti and nearby islands; Philip Carteret visits Pitcairn Island and New Ireland.

1768
James Cook carries out scientific work near Tahiti.

1769–1770
Cook circumnavigates New Zealand.

1770
Cook sails up the east coast of Australia.

1772–1775

Cook visits or sights Vanuatu, the Marquesas, Tonga, New Caledonia, and many more Pacific Islands on his second Pacific expedition.

1778

Cook first visits the Hawaiian Islands.

1779

Cook is killed in Hawaii.

1798–1799

Matthew Flinders proves that Tasmania is an island.

1803

Flinders completes circumnavigation of Australia.

1813

Gregory Blaxland crosses the Blue Mountains.

1824

Hamilton Hume and William Hovell cross southeastern Australia.

1828–1829

Hume and Charles Sturt reach the Darling River.

1830

Sturt journeys down the Murrumbidgee and Murray rivers.

1839

Edward Eyre journeys into the Australian interior.

1839–1840

Henry Williams explores the interior of New Zealand's South Island.

1841

Eyre travels the southern coast of Australia by land.

1845

Sturt reaches Cooper's Creek.

1860

Robert Burke sets off from Adelaide to cross Australia.

1861

Burke and three companions reach Australia's northern coast; Burke and two companions die on the trip back to Adelaide.

1862

John McDouall Stuart completes round-trip crossing of Australia.

For Further Reading

Books

Stephen Currie, *Polynesians*. Mankato, MN: Smart Apple Media, 2000. A brief account of the people of Polynesia today and through history, including information on early exploration by the Polynesians themselves.

Vijeya and Sundran Rajendia, *Australia*. New York: Benchmark Books, 2002. A detailed description of the history, peoples, and land of Australia.

David Sommerville, *Australia and Asia*. Danbury, CT: Grolier Educational, 1998. A simply written and well-illustrated book on the exploration of Australia and parts of Asia.

Rebecca Stefoff, *Ferdinand Magellan and the Discovery of the World Ocean*. New York: Chelsea House, 1990. About Magellan and his circumnavigation of the earth; includes useful information about the reasons for early Spanish and Portuguese explorations as well as on Magellan's trip across the Pacific.

Oliver Warner, *Captain Cook and the South Pacific*. New York: American Heritage, 1963. Well-illustrated and informative. Gives excellent background on Cook, the progress of expeditions before Cook's time, and Cook's three Pacific voyages.

Jean Kinney Williams, *Cook: James Cook Charts the Pacific Ocean*. Minneapolis, MN: Compass Point Books, 2003. A short but useful account of Cook's voyages.

C.H. Wright, *Exploring the Continent*. Melbourne, Australia: F.W. Cheshire, 1960. A somewhat breathless but informative description of Australia's exploration.

Web Sites

BBCi, "Exploration" (www.bbc.co.uk/history/discovery/exploration). A compilation of articles about the history of exploration, including several articles about the Pacific, Cook and his life and work, and several other topics of interest.

Polynesian Voyaging Society (www.leahi.kcc.hawaii.edu/org/pvs). Provides detailed information on early Polynesian migrations and exploration.

Trinity College Western Australia, "Australian Explorers" (www.library.trinity.wa.edu.au/subjects/sose/austhist/austexp.htm). Provides links to many pages with time lines, profiles, and detailed information on the exploration of Australia, both by sea and by land.

Works Consulted

Oliver E. Allen, *The Pacific Navigators.* Alexandria, VA: Time-Life, 1980. A beautifully illustrated and well-researched account of Pacific exploration through the time of James Cook.

K.A. Austin, *The Voyage of the Investigator.* Adelaide, Australia: Rigby, 1964. Describes Matthew Flinders's circumnavigation of Australia, including a number of extracts from the journals of Flinders and his crew.

Michael Barone and Grant Ujifusa, *The American Almanac of Politics 2000.* Washington, DC: National Journal, 1999. Useful for information about Hawaii, Guam, and American Samoa.

Peter Bellwood, *The Polynesians.* London: Thames and Hudson, 1978. Discusses the prehistory of the central and western Pacific, including information on early Polynesian voyagers. Part of a series called Ancient People and Places.

Roderick Cameron, *Australia: History and Horizons.* New York: Columbia University Press, 1971. A solid general history of Australia, though selective in its description of expeditions.

———, *The Golden Haze.* Cleveland: World, 1964. Cameron visited many of the places explored by James Cook. This book combines his own experiences and observations with the accounts of Cook and his men.

Johann Reinhold Forster, *The Resolution Journal of Johann Reinhold Forster.* London: Hakluyt Society, 1982. Forster was a naturalist who traveled on Cook's second expedition. This four-volume set includes commentary and Forster's own observations and experiences during the trip.

Hakluyt Society, *The Discovery of the Solomon Islands.* London: Hakluyt Society, 1891. Accounts from Mendaña and several other explorers relating to the Spanish voyage to Santa Isabel and Guadalcanal.

David Howarth, *Tahiti: A Paradise Lost.* New York: Viking Press, 1983. A history of Tahiti from Wallis's expedition on. Useful information about Wallis and Cook. Howarth's main interest, though, is in the effects of contact between Europeans and Tahitians.

Neil M. Levy, *Micronesia Handbook.* Emeryville, CA: Avalon Travel, 1985. A travel guide including useful basic history of Micronesia and its islands.

David Lewis, *The Voyaging Stars.* New York: W.W. Norton, 1978. Lewis describes the methods of navigation used among Pacific Islanders today as well as historically. He is a strong advocate for the idea that early Polynesian explorers were fully aware of where they were going.

Alan Moorehead, *Cooper's Creek*. New York: Harper and Row, 1963. An account of the Burke-Wills expedition.

————, *The Fatal Impact*. New York: Harper and Row, 1966. About Captain Cook's voyages to Tahiti, Australia, and the Antarctic and the changes they brought to the people of the Pacific. Also includes information on several other important explorers and expeditions.

Ian Mudie, *The Heroic Journey of John McDouall Stuart*. Sydney, Australia: Angus Robertson, 1968. A thorough account of Stuart's trek across the Australian continent.

Sarah Murgatroyd, *The Dig Tree*. New York: Broadway, 2002. The story of the Burke expedition into Australia's Outback. Interesting and informative. Murgatroyd sees Burke as a typical English explorer of the time—long on courage and short on ability.

Piers Pennington, *The Great Explorers*. New York: Facts On File, 1979. Accounts of many great explorers and expeditions through history, including descriptions of the voyages of Cook, Tasman, Flinders, and others.

Antonio Pigafetta, *The First Voyage Around the World*. New York: Marsilio, 1995. Pigafetta was a sailor who accompanied Magellan on his first circumnavigation of the globe. This book is the account of that voyage.

George Robertson, *The Discovery of Tahiti*. London: Hakluyt Society, 1948. Robertson was aboard the *Dolphin* with Samuel Wallis when it first sighted Tahiti. This is Robertson's account of the voyage.

Andrew Sharp, *Ancient Voyagers in Polynesia*. London: Angus Robertson, 1964. This book examines the remarkable ability of Polynesians to navigate and theorizes about how Polynesia may have been settled. Sharp's thesis is that Polynesian exploration was less purposeful than generally believed.

————, *The Discovery of Australia*. Oxford, England: Clarendon Press, 1963. Documents and explanatory materials dealing with sea voyages to Australia.

Keith Sinclair, *A History of New Zealand*. London: Oxford University Press, 1961. Includes some basic information on Cook and Tasman; Sinclair is more interested, however, in political history through the years.

John W. Wright, ed., *2004 New York Times Almanac*. New York: New York Times, 2003. Maps, facts, and figures about Australia and the Pacific Islands, both today and in the past.

Index

Picture Credits

About the Author

Stephen Currie is the creator of Lucent's Discovery and Exploration series. He also originated Lucent's Great Escapes series, and has published many other books and articles as well. He lives with his family in New York State. His interests include hiking and kayaking, although his skills in these areas do not begin to approach those of the first Polynesian settlers or the Europeans who explored Australia's interior.